A Continual Feast

*Recipes for Food,
Inspiratation for Life*

Debra Brawner

WestBow
PRESS
A DIVISION OF THOMAS NELSON

All Scripture quotations are taken from the King James Version of the Bible.

*Chicago: Simon & Garfunkel - I Am A Rock Lyrics, http://artists.letssingit.com/ simon-garfunkel-lyrics-i-am-a-rock-q5wgvx1 (accessed September 26, 2010).

WestBow Press books may be ordered through booksellers or by contacting:

WestBow Press
A Division of Thomas Nelson
1663 Liberty Drive
Bloomington, IN 47403
www.westbowpress.com
1-(866) 928-1240

ISBN: 978-1-4497-3995-9 (sc)
ISBN: 978-1-4497-3996-6 (hc)
ISBN: 978-1-4497-3994-2 (e)

Library of Congress Control Number: 2012902241

Printed in the United States of America

WestBow Press rev. date: 04/05/2012

To my daughter, Rebekah Kay Brawner. I love that through the trials and hardships of life's journey, you are learning to trust God's grace. I see you becoming a woman of destiny and purpose. May we enjoy many more years of cooking and laughing together. I pray that out of the fullness of His grace you receive blessing upon blessing (John 1:16).

To my sisters, Janean Lee and Mary Ann McCulloch, who have loved, encouraged, and supported me all my life. You are an inspiration. I enjoy our many lunches and laughter together. You are far more precious than jewels, and your value is far above rubies. (Proverbs 31:10).

"He that has a merry heart has a continual feast."—Proverbs 15:15

Contents

Foreword

Debra Brawner has beautifully illustrated in her stories, biblical wisdom, and family-pleasing recipes that the art of cooking is not lost. Our ever-present time crunch and the availability of restaurants and prepared foods have led many people straight out of the kitchen; but Debra gently leads us right back into the pleasure of cooking. She stirs not only the comforting pot of soup, but our souls as well. She cooks up far more than delicious food, but nourishment that satisfies and strengthens the soul and spirit.

I love her tour through the biblical fruits of the Spirit and the recipes they inspired. Here is a book that showcases the heart of God toward us with a practical guide to good food. God creates the fruit and then puts it into the hands of people like Debra, who prepare it and dish it out to a hurting world.

It is wonderful to observe and experience the fruit of the Spirit growing in a person. It produces a renewed heart, a different way of thinking, and good will toward God and people. That is a recipe for happiness and fulfilled destiny, and it is obtainable for each of us as we receive God's love and learn His ways. These wonders are served up within these pages.

Dianne Davis
Southwest US Director, Aglow International

Acknowledgments

A special thanks to my grand-niece, Hailey McCulloch. Your help with editing and your encouraging words were invaluable. What a delightful young woman you are!

With much appreciation, I thank Dr. Cathy Smades for your guidance and encouragement in writing this cookbook. I am eternally grateful for your leadership as my pastor. What a difference you have made in my life with your wisdom and understanding. Thank you for being a lover of people and a head over heels lover of Jesus Christ. You are an inspiration to me.

Chapter One

Cooking and Living with Flavor

The crunchy, juicy bite of an apple; the sweet, watery taste of watermelon; the aroma and sweet tang of an orange—fruit can be refreshing, invigorating, and thoroughly enjoyable. The benefits of fruit are numerous. Eating fruit can offset a diet of processed foods, which tends to rob our bodies of nutrients instead of supplying them. Eating fruit provides nourishment of many needed vitamins, minerals, enzymes, and antioxidants.

Vitamin A, found in cantaloupe, helps prevent eye diseases and premature wrinkles. Oranges, mangoes, and other fruits contain vitamin C, which protects the body from skin diseases, respiratory infections, and cardiovascular problems. It also helps with growth and repair of tissue. Lycopene, found in watermelon and pink grapefruit, cleanses the blood and helps prevent tumors and cancer. Flavonoids, also called vitamin P or citron, found in grapes, protect against heart disease. Many fruits, such as apples, berries, and dried fruit, contain soluble fiber that helps the digestive system and regulates cholesterol levels. Potassium, found in bananas, helps lower blood pressure and water retention.

Free radicals bring oxygen to our cells, causing damage to them. Antioxidants prevent this cell damage by neutralizing the free radicals. Vitamins, minerals, and enzymes work together for optimum health, slowing down the aging process, boosting natural energy, and helping to prevent diseases. Experts say that if one-third of a diet consists of fruits and vegetables, weight loss occurs. Eating fruit helps people to feel better physically. When feeling better physically, we feel better emotionally and mentally.

Some processed foods provide excellent nutrition, such as frozen fruit and vegetables, but most do not. They strip the body of needed nutrients, which guard against disease. In a similar way, there are many things that rob our souls of health: bitterness, anger, resentment, and fears, to name a few. Eating natural foods brings nourishment, providing health and energy in the same way that focusing thoughts on positive things bring us inner contentment.

People know how to apply natural food to natural bodies to get the optimum benefits, but what about applying spiritual food to one's spirit? Humans live in a body and have a soul (mind, will, and emotions) and a spirit (the deep place in us that God inhabits). In Hebrews 4:12, Saint Paul talks about the Word of God being alive and more powerful and sharper than a two-edged sword. It separates the soul from the spirit, the joints, and marrow, and it discerns the thoughts and intent of the heart. Teaching the soul to be a vehicle of the spirit requires work. These two parts battle for control of who we are.

The soul of man fights to be in control. It wants self-gratification and resists God. It does not understand God or His ways. It is finite and limited. The soul does not easily surrender to God, but there are keys to help it get there.

The first step to bringing life to our spirits is to invite Jesus into our lives. After we come to Christ, our spirit man comes alive, and then comes the battle for control between the soul and the spirit. Soul power must be broken if we are going to serve God effectively. Peace and contentment is only found when the soul becomes a vehicle for our spirits to operate. In 1 Thessalonians 5:23, Saint Paul states, "The very God of peace sanctify you wholly; and I pray God your whole spirit and soul and body be preserved blameless unto the coming of our Lord Jesus Christ."

There may be reasons people have heart trouble—smoking, drinking, heredity, diet, and lack of exercise. Just as people need to eat plenty of fruit and vegetables, exercise, and practice a healthy lifestyle in order to have a healthy heart, a healthy soul and spirit requires right thinking, good attitude, and studying God's Word and putting it into practice.

In Ezekiel 36:26–27, God tells us, "A new heart also will I give you, and a new spirit will I put within you: and I will take away the stony heart out of your flesh, and I will give you a heart of flesh. I will put my spirit within you, and cause you to walk in my statutes, and ye shall keep my judgments, and do them."

Sometimes people need a heart transplant because their physical heart arteries have become clogged and their hearts cannot pump blood. When blood does not flow through the heart, there is no life. Just as it is possible to get a new heart for one's body, one can acquire a new heart for one's spirit. Sin separates us from a loving, caring God. Only He can give a new spiritual heart. He sent Jesus, His only begotten Son, who spilled his own blood for all and became sin, in exchange for all to have the right standing with God. When God gives a new heart, that person becomes a citizen of heaven living from a different perspective. No longer captive to living only from an earthly viewpoint, one can learn to live heaven to earth. Experiencing the fruit of the Spirit requires a renewed heart and changed mind. It takes constant practice.

The fruit of the Spirit reveals the nature of God. Sometimes life is dark and grim. God desires to show His capability to free us from all fear and anxiety. Each circumstance is a growth opportunity designed to draw us closer to God and experience His true nature of love. Drawing closer to God produces the fruit of love, joy, and peace. A new spiritual heart grows as a result of this new life. A heart of stone—an unforgiving, self-centered, unresponsive heart—is replaced with a tender, soft heart. It takes a relationship and friendship with the Holy Spirit through faith. Allowing the Spirit of Christ to live in one's heart creates an inward change, which in turn causes an outward change in behavior.

Galatians 5:13–16 states, "For, brethren, ye have been called unto liberty; only use not liberty for an occasion to the flesh, but by love serve one another. For all the law is fulfilled in one word, even in this; Thou shalt love thy neighbor as thyself. But if ye bite and devour one another, take heed that ye are not consumed one of another. This I say then, Walk in the Spirit, and ye shall not fulfill the lust of the flesh."

The exciting news is that God just wants us to love each other. Love brings liberty. Biting and devouring others with words and actions hurts others, but it hurts the perpetrator even more. Living this way takes up too much energy and time and brings destruction instead of life. Inflicting hurt and pain on others has a boomerang effect, coming back to you with anxiety, depression, and hopelessness. Determination to live a life of love and acceptance will reap the rewards of peace and joy. The best remedy against anger, resentment, and bitterness is walking and living in love. Living in the Spirit is a lifestyle that takes practice and adds exceptional flavor to lives.

Sunshine, nutrition, water, and fresh air help produce fruit. There is nothing more delicious than fresh fruit. It satisfies as it energizes and delights the body and soul. Just as an apple is grown by living on an apple tree, the fruit of the Spirit is developed by abiding in Christ, by planting His Word in our hearts and acting on it. We learn to change.

Instead of anger, we produce love. Instead of turmoil, we produce peace. Instead of sorrow, we produce joy. Instead of impatience, we produce patience. We produce gentleness in place of harshness. Goodness replaces selfishness. Instead of being unstable, we become faithful. Weakness becomes meekness. Lack of control becomes self-control.

God's commandments can only be fulfilled by love. Knowing Him, loving Him, following Him, and imitating Him produces the fruit mentioned in the Bible. "But the fruit of the Spirit is love, joy, peace, longsuffering, gentleness, goodness, faithfulness, meekness, temperance: against such there is no law" (Galatians 5:22–23). Practicing these things makes life flavorful.

Love

There is no other commandment greater than to love God and to love others as you love yourself. Love does no harm to others, which fully satisfies God's requirements. This is the foundation of all the commandments. When practicing the law of love, there is no desire to harm or hurt others. If everyone sought to love, all the commandments would be fulfilled. Love requires that we pursue the good of others (Matthew 22:37–40).

Joy

Rejoicing is at the heart of life with Christ. When troubles are more than we can be bear, and life does not make sense, choose to praise God. This is where real strength is created. When all else is gone, God is still here. Hearts become enlarged so we can walk ahead of troubles (Habakkuk 3:17–19).

Peace

The Word of God offers what nothing else can: peace, or a sense of complete well-being. Stability and calmness of mind and emotions comes from trusting God and His Word.—it also provides help for today, hope for tomorrow and growth in confidence. He promises deliverance from fear, and this freedom makes us complete (Psalm 91).

Longsuffering/Patience

God is a master at turning hard and impossible situations into something beautiful. No matter the difficulties, we have a promise that, in all things, God works for the good of those who love Him and have been called according to His purpose. His followers don't just overcome adversity, but they are also given lives of favor, and their natures are transformed into the character of Christ. Never giving up or giving in, triumphing in the end, they rejoice. Learning to wait on His timing enables His children to triumph in every situation (Romans 8:28–29).

Gentleness

The opposite of being controlling and self-centered is gentleness. It stems from trusting in God's goodness and control over every situation. A gentle person is not preoccupied with having to control life's situations or others, but has learned to relinquish it all to a loving God. This is the work of the Holy Spirit, not the human will (1 Peter 3:4).

Goodness

Knowing and experiencing the goodness of God leaves one with a taste for more. He is full of grace, kindness, and mercy. Just as eating wholesome, nourishing food produces life and a healthy body, meditating on God's Word nourishes a person's spirit and brings a deeper understanding of the grace and favor found in Christ. Drawing near to God guarantees that He will draw near to those who seek Him. Experiencing God's goodness causes growth in goodness expressed toward others (1 Peter 2:3).

Faithfulness

In faithfulness, God established the heavens and the earth. He spoke a word, and it was done. He formed mankind from the dust of the earth, and then with the breath from His own mouth, He gave him life and created mankind. Mankind has been His most loved and special creation ever since. Nothing can separate people from His love. No matter what they may have done, nothing can change His love. He is eager to forgive. Christ died for the sin of all. Judgment has been dealt with once for all. He faithfully watches out for those who trust Him. Rescuing and delivering, He never gives up on His seekers. His faithfulness never sways, even when His people do. He will never leave them or forsake them (Psalm 33:18–22).

Meekness

The meek have learned a secret; they have learned to trust and rely on God and His strength. They know that, in the end, they will win the good fight of faith and all will work out for their good. They know that whatever they are presently going through is only temporary and will pass. God is in control. Through the troubles of life, the meek have peace, fresh joy, and strength because they know where to find the help they need. Having confidence, they know that one day God's faithfulness and promises will triumph (Isaiah 29:19).

Temperance/Self-Control

The inability to control our impulses or passions drains us of all that is good. Being out of control in certain areas of our lives may cause us to overcompensate and be over-controlling in other areas: this can result in controlling and manipulating behaviors that may make us feel that we have power, but actually create unfruitful relationships. As we learn to walk with Christ, we learn to rule and reign in ways that produce the fruit of the spirit (Proverbs 16:32).

Chapter Two

Love and Potlucks

As an adolescent, I would sit in my bedroom and sing Simon and Garfunkel's song, *"I Am A Rock." It goes, "I am a rock. I am an island. A rock feels no pain. An island never cries." Wanting to be independent, I tried to convince myself that I did not need anyone. I could do it by myself. It did not take long to find out that I really didn't like being alone. Choosing to take down my walls allowed me to open up to love. Thinking that I did not need others made it impossible to love others and to be loved. We were created to have relationships. That is what makes life worthwhile.

Life has a way of presenting people with hurts and pains that make them feel hardened and self-protective. When nothing is getting better, there is a choice to be made. We can choose to draw nearer to God, or we can surrender to the negativity and become even more isolated. Hurt and pain happens to us all. We may be tempted to lash out at God and accuse Him of not loving us.

This is the time when He wants most to reveal Himself as the one who loves us and will never forsake us. He wants to comfort us in the midst of our painful situations. He will heal the hurts and pains and enable His followers to love when they feel incapable. Open your heart to Him, and He will reveal Himself. You will experience love in deeper ways then you ever imagined and enjoy a renewed heart, a different way of thinking, and growth in the fruit of the Spirit.

The foundation of Christianity is love—love for God and others. All displays of Christianity fall short if love is not demonstrated first and foremost. "They will know you are my followers if you love one another." Love never fails, and its consequences last throughout eternity.

"Though I speak with the tongues of men and of angels, and have not charity (love), I am become as sounding brass or a tinkling cymbal. Though I have the gift of prophecy, and understand all mysteries, and all knowledge; and though I have all faith, so that I could remove mountains, and have not charity, I am nothing. Though I bestow all my goods to feed the poor, and though I give my body to be burned, and have not charity, it profiteth me nothing. Charity suffereth long, and is kind; charity envieth not; charity vaunteth not itself, is not puffed up, Doth not behave itself unseemly, seeketh not her own, is not easily provoked, thinketh no evil; Rejoices not in iniquity, but rejoiceth in the truth; Beareth all things, believeth all things, hopeth all things, endureth all things. Charity never faileth. And now abideth faith, hope, charity, these three; but the greatest of these is charity" (1 Cor. 13:1–13).

Prayer

Jesus, I choose to love, for love is a choice and an action, just not a feeling. You, Lord, are the source of love. I ask you to give me the power to love. Teach me, how to show love to others, even the difficult. Father, thank you for demonstrating how much you loved us by sending your only Son into this fallen world. His love brought us eternal life through His death and resurrection. By this act, we see what real love is. We love you because you first loved us. Amen (I John 4:8–9).

Potluck, or as some call it, pot blessings, reminds me of the fruit of love. For centuries the church has celebrated love feasts where members would come together and share their food as tokens of brotherly love, in the same way we do today. It is a special time to celebrate friendships and families.

Potluck Recipes

Green Bean and Egg Casserole

1 9-ounce package frozen green beans
¼ cup butter
¼ cup minced onions
¼ cup flour
2 cups milk
2 teaspoons salt
2 teaspoons black pepper
2 teaspoons thyme
1 tablespoon dried parsley
6 hard-boiled eggs, chopped
½ cup dry bread crumbs
½ cup shredded Swiss cheese

Preheat oven to 350 °F. Cook beans according to package directions and drain. In a large pan, melt butter and sauté onions. Stir in flour and gradually add milk. Cook, stirring constantly, until sauce is thick and smooth. Add seasonings and parsley. Grease casserole dish and fill with alternate layers of beans, eggs, and sauce. Sprinkle top layer with crumbs mixed with cheese. Bake for 20 to 25 minutes.

Stuffed Mushrooms

20 large fresh mushrooms
1 teaspoon vegetable oil
½ pound ground sirloin
2 cloves of garlic, minced
8 ounces cream cheese, softened
3 cup shredded cheddar cheese
½ teaspoon black pepper
½ teaspoon onion powder

Preheat oven to 350 °F. Spray a cookie sheet with cooking spray. Clean mushrooms with a damp paper towel, gently remove the stems and cut them into fine pieces. In a twelve-inch skillet, heat oil over medium heat. Add meat, garlic, and mushroom stems. Cook until meat is thoroughly cooked. Set aside to cool. Stir in cream cheese, cheddar cheese, pepper, and onion powder.

Using a small spoon, generously fill each mushroom with the mixture. Arrange mushroom caps on cooking sheet. Bake for 15 to 20 minutes, until liquid starts to form under the caps.

Spaghetti Salad

4 cups cooked spaghetti
½ cup green onions, chopped
½ cup tomatoes, chopped
½ cup green peppers, chopped
½ cup black olives, chopped
½ cup cheddar cheese, shredded
¼ cup Parmesan cheese
½ cup Italian dressing

In a large bowl, mix all ingredients. Chill in the refrigerator for at least two hours before serving.

Bean Lasagna Bake

1 onion, chopped
2 cloves garlic, minced
1 green pepper, chopped
1 15-ounce can black beans, drained and rinsed
1 15-ounce can chili beans, drained and rinsed
1 26-ounce can crushed tomatoes, not drained
1 cup salsa
2 tablespoons chili powder
1 teaspoon cumin
2 cups ricotta cheese
1 egg, beaten
¾ cup Parmesan cheese
10–12 uncooked lasagna noodles
2 cups shredded mozzarella cheese

Preheat oven to 350 °F. In a medium pan, sauté the onion, garlic, and green pepper. Set aside to cool. In a large bowl, combine onion, garlic, green pepper, beans, tomatoes, salsa, chili powder, and cumin. In a small bowl, combine ricotta cheese, egg, and ½ cup Parmesan cheese. Mix well. In 13 x 9-inch baking dish, spread one cup of tomato and bean mixture. Follow with half the noodles, breaking the noodles as necessary to fit. Add a layer with half the remaining tomato and bean mixture. Spread the ricotta mixture over the top. Sprinkle with ½ cup mozzarella cheese. Add the remaining noodles and tomato mixture. Top with remaining mozzarella cheese and ¼ cup Parmesan cheese.

Cover baking dish and bake for 55 minutes or until noodles are tender. Uncover and bake for another 10 minutes, until casserole is bubbling and cheese begins to brown.

Baked Ham

1 12-pound bone-in ham, rump portion
½ cup whole cloves
1 cup packed brown sugar
2 teaspoons black pepper
1 16-ounce can sliced pineapple
4 cups water, or as much as needed

Preheat the oven to 350 °F. Place ham in a roasting pan. Pour juice from pineapples on ham. Press the top of ham with a mixture of pepper and brown sugar. Place pineapple slices on top. If needed, secure with toothpicks. Press whole cloves into the top at 1- to 2-inch intervals. Fill the bottom of the roasting pan with one inch of water. Cover the pan with aluminum foil or a lid. Bake the ham for 4 ½ to 5 hours or until the internal temperature of the ham has reached 160 degrees. Remove any toothpicks. Let stand for about 20 minutes before carving.

Steak and Vegetables

6 carrots, thinly sliced diagonally
4 cups water
1 pound chuck steak, partially frozen, sliced very thinly
4 tablespoons butter
2 garlic cloves, chopped
1 10-ounce package frozen Italian green beans
1 onion, thinly sliced
½ teaspoon salt
4 cups cooked, buttered rice
Soy sauce to taste

In an eight-inch pan, bring water to a boil. Add carrots, cover, and boil over medium heat for 5 minutes. In a twelve-inch skillet, heat butter with garlic and add steak. Cook over medium-high heat until well browned on both sides. Move to a warm platter. Add the carrots and green beans to the skillet drippings. Cook until vegetables are tender, about 10 minutes, and then add onions and meat. Continue cooking until onions are tender, about 5 minutes, and then sprinkle with salt. Place the rice on a large serving tray. Put the meat and vegetables on top and sprinkle with soy sauce.

Ground Beef and Hominy

2 16-ounce cans of golden hominy, drained
2 cups condensed tomato soup
1 cup chopped black olives
1 teaspoon salt
1 teaspoon chili powder
1 teaspoon garlic salt
½ teaspoon black pepper
2 pounds ground beef or ground turkey
1 large onion, chopped
1 cup celery, chopped
½ cup green pepper, chopped
1 cup Parmesan cheese, grated

Preheat oven to 375°F. In a large mixing bowl, combine hominy, tomato soup, olives, garlic salt, chili powder, and pepper. Set aside. In a twelve-inch skillet, sauté ground beef, onion, celery, and green pepper. Combine hominy mixture with meat mixture and turn into a greased baking dish. Bake 30 minutes. Top with cheese and bake 5 minutes longer.

Apple Cake

2 large eggs
2 teaspoons sugar
1 cup salad oil
1 teaspoon nutmeg
1 teaspoon salt
1 teaspoon baking soda
1 teaspoon vanilla
2 cups sifted flour
2 cups peeled, cored, and chopped apples
1 cup chopped walnuts

Preheat the oven to 350 °F. In a large mixing bowl, beat the eggs. Add sugar and mix well with an electric beater. Add oil, cinnamon, nutmeg, salt, baking soda, and vanilla. Slowly add the flour and then the apple and walnuts. Pour into a well-greased 9 x 13-inch pan. Bake for 55 minutes.

100 Cookies

1 cup brown sugar
1 cup sugar
1 cup oil
1 cup butter
3 ½ cups all purpose flour
1 teaspoon cream of tartar
1 teaspoon salt
1 cup coconut
1 egg
1 cup crispy rice cereal
2 teaspoons vanilla
1 cup oatmeal
1 teaspoon baking soda
1 12-ounce package semi-sweet chocolate chips

Preheat oven to 350 °F. Cream the sugars, oil, and butter. Add the flour. Mix the remaining ingredients in the order given. Form into 100 balls and place them on cookie sheets. Bake 10 to 12 minutes. Place on cookie sheet and bake 10-12 minutes.

Chapter Three

Joy and Fruit

Both of my parents suffered from depression. Some of the symptoms they displayed were irritability, nervousness, moodiness, difficulty sleeping, feelings of hopelessness, chronic fatigue, social isolation, and outbursts of anger. It is no surprise that I also suffered from these things. As I learned to follow Jesus, I discovered that He was a man of immense joy. He was the most cheerful person who ever lived. "He was anointed with the oil of gladness above His fellows" (Hebrews 1:9). The gladness and joy He carried with Him drew others and was contagious. He was a great delight to be around and brought joy with Him wherever He went.

I do not mean to simplify the cure for depression, but I decided that I would devote myself to finding joy in life. I printed out all the scriptures on joy and read and meditated on them every day. Joy gives strength and energy. It brings health. "A merry heart doeth good like a medicine: but a broken spirit drieth the bones" (Proverbs 17: 22). Depression robs us of having full, prosperous lives. There is no way to experience the abundant life that Jesus promises if there is no joy.

Life can be difficult, painful, unpredictable, uncontrollable, and full of heartache. Knowing that God designs every problem with provision can give us hope. Hope energizes and gives joy. Jesus desires to turn every affliction into His glory, where we end up on top. His resurrection from the dead is the source of hope and great encouragement to those who once were hopeless and full of despair.

People can experience joy and happiness no matter what is happening. Jesus taught us to pray, "On earth as it is in heaven." In heaven, there is only joy, laughter, and love. Jesus came to give us joy. He showed that no matter what the circumstance, He always had joy, even when He was facing death on the cross (Hebrews 12:2). No one could take the joy from Him. When believers realize this, they experience the same kind of joy. They gain strength and power. Learning to live from their spirits, they experience the pleasure of becoming more like Christ in all aspects. Not only is God able, but He also delights in making every situation work for the good. Now that is reason to rejoice!

Jesus proclaimed His mission the first time He publicly preached. "The Spirit of the Lord God is upon me; because the Lord hath anointed me to preach good tidings unto the meek; he hath sent me to bind up the brokenhearted, to proclaim liberty to the captives, and the opening of the prison to them that are bound; To proclaim the acceptable year of the LORD" (Luke 4: 18–19). Good news—He came to heal the broken-hearted and deliver them from evil. He proclaimed freedom. He gives beauty instead of sorrow, joy instead of mourning, and instead of depression He gives praise. Praise produces joy. Joy gives power and strength. Joy and praise go hand in hand.

Prayer

Jesus, fill me with joy as I trust in you. You are abundantly good. Glorify yourself in my life. Cause me to rejoice because every problem comes with a provision. Teach me to live in the power of joy. Cause me to be a person who brings joy with me wherever I go. Amen.

Recipes that involve fruit remind me of joy. I remember as a child the anticipation and excitement I felt when watermelon was in season. I always looked forward to eating it. I felt the same way about strawberries. Each spring my grade school had a strawberry festival. The main feature was strawberry shortcake. Excitement and anticipation filled the children as we looked forward to the festival and eating strawberry shortcake. Every one of my schoolmates looked forward to the event. When I look back on it, I can see that it brought us so much joy as we relished each bite of strawberry shortcake.

Fruit Recipes

Fruit Smoothie

1 6-ounce container strawberry yogurt
½ cup strawberries, fresh or frozen
1 ripe banana
½ cup apple juice
¼ cup uncooked oatmeal
1 cup ice

In a blender, combine yogurt, strawberries, banana, apple juice, oatmeal, and ice. Cover and blend on medium speed for about 2 minutes or until smooth. Pour into a serving glass. There are many variations of fruit smoothies and numerous ways to make them. It is fun to experiment with smoothies by combining different fruit together and discover interesting flavors. For extra nutrition, add fresh or frozen berries.

Serves one

Glazed Fresh Strawberry Pie

1 premade baked 9-inch pie crust
6 cups fresh strawberries, hulled
1 cup water
2 tablespoons cornstarch
2 tablespoons cold water
¼ cup sugar
Whipped topping if desired

Place 1¼ cup strawberries and 1 cup of water in a food processor or blender, cover and blend until mixture is smooth. Transfer to a small saucepan, bring to a boil, and simmer for 2 minutes. In a separate bowl, whisk together the cornstarch and 2 tablespoons of water until cornstarch is dissolved. Add the sugar and then stir into the blended strawberry mixture. Stir over medium heat until mixture is thickened and bubbly. Continue to cook and stir for 2 more minutes. Remove from heat and cool to room temperature. After it's cooled, fold in remaining strawberries and pour into baked pie shell. Cover and refrigerate 3 to 4 hours or until set. Serve with whipped topping, if desired.

Serves six

Fresh Applesauce

8 cooking apples, peeled, cored, and chopped
½ cup sugar
½ teaspoon cinnamon
½ cup water

In a saucepan, combine the apples, sugar, cinnamon, and water. Cover and cook over medium heat for about 15 minutes. Allow to cool to warm. Mash with a fork or potato masher. Cool and refrigerate one to two hours.

Serves six

Banana Bread

1¾ cup all-purpose flour
⅔ cup sugar
1 teaspoon baking powder
½ teaspoon salt
¼ teaspoon baking soda
½ cup butter, softened
1 cup mashed banana (approximately 2 very ripe medium bananas)
2 eggs, slightly beaten
1 teaspoon vanilla extract
½ cup coarsely chopped pecans or walnuts

Preheat oven to 350 °F. Grease and flour 9 by 5-inch loaf pan. In a large bowl, mix flour, sugar, baking powder, salt, and baking soda with a spoon. With pastry blender or two knives used scissor-fashion, cut in butter until mixture resembles coarse crumbs. Stir in bananas, vanilla, eggs, and nuts until just blended and spread batter evenly into loaf pan. Bake 55 minutes to an hour until toothpick inserted in center comes out clean. Cool on wire rack. Remove from pan and cool completely.

Serves eight

Fruit Salad

1 small head romaine lettuce
1 small honeydew melon
1 small cantaloupe
1 pint strawberries
2 small seedless oranges
2 small avocados
2 tablespoons lemon juice
½ pound seedless green grapes
½ pound seedless red grapes
Mint Creme Dip-Recipe on following page

Separate, wash, and dry romaine leaves and set aside. Halve the honeydew, scoop out the seeds, and cut it into balls with a melon ball cutter or a ½ teaspoon. Do the same thing with the cantaloupe. Wash the strawberries, hull and halve them. Peel oranges and cut into slices. Quarter avocados and remove pits; brush with lemon juice to keep color bright.

To arrange the platter, line a serving bowl with romaine leaves. Stand the avocado quarters in front of romaine. Set the dressing bowl in front of avocados to hold them in place. Arrange the rest of the fruit around the dressing bowl. Spoon the mint-cream dressing into dressing bowl.

Mint Cream Dip

1 cup sour cream
3 tablespoons chopped fresh mint
2 tablespoons confectioner's sugar
¼ teaspoon cardamom

In a small bowl, blend the sour cream, mint, confectioner's sugar and cardamom, cover, and refrigerate for at least 30 minutes.

Serves eight

Raspberry Pretzel Delight

Crust:

1 ½ cups crushed pretzels (a food processor or blender works well or pretzels can be placed in a plastic bag and crushed with a rolling pin.)
¼ cup sugar
½ cup melted butter or margarine

Filling:

1 12-ounce can sweetened condensed milk
½ cup water
1 ¾-ounce package instant vanilla pudding and pie filling
1 4-ounce carton light whipping cream, whipped

Topping;
1 21-ounce can raspberry fruit pie filling
(blueberry or cherry fruit pie filling can be substituted)

Preheat oven to 350 °F. In a large bowl, combine crushed pretzels, sugar, and butter. Press into the bottom of an ungreased 9 x 13-inch pan. Bake for 8 minutes and then set aside to cool. In another bowl, add condensed milk and water and blend well. Add pudding mix and beat for 2 minutes. Refrigerate for 5 minutes and then fold in about three quarters of the whipped topping. Spread on to the baked crust and refrigerate about one hour. Spoon whipped topping over filling and cover. Keep refrigerated until ready to serve. Garnish with fresh raspberries and mint leaves, if desired.

Serves eight

Chocolate Fondue

4 4-ounce bars unsweetened baking chocolate, broken into pieces
1 cup light cream
1 cup sugar
¼ cup creamy peanut butter
1½ teaspoons vanilla extract
Assorted fondue dippers, such as cherries, grapes, bananas, pineapple chunks, strawberries, apple slices, and grapes

In a medium saucepan, warm the cream until it just starts to bubble. Add the chocolate and cook over low heat, whisking constantly until chocolate melts and mixture is smooth. Stir in sugar and peanut butter and continue cooking until slightly thickened, stirring constantly. Remove from heat. Stir in vanilla and pour into fondue pot or chafing dish. Serve with assorted fondue dippers.

Serves eight

Pineapple Upside-Down Cake

2 tablespoons butter
½ cup brown sugar
4 slices of canned pineapple
7 Maraschino cherries
1 18-ounce box yellow cake mix

Preheat oven to 325 °F. Melt butter and pour into a 9 x 13-inch pan. Blend in sugar. Place pineapple slices and cherries in pan. Prepare cake mix batter according to package directions using pineapple juice for liquid. Add water if needed. Pour batter over fruit. Bake about 45 minutes or until toothpick inserted in center comes out clean. Let cool completely before serving.

Serves eight

Creamy Fruit Delight

1 8-ounce package cream cheese, softened
½ cup canned peach baby food
½ teaspoon ginger
½ teaspoon nutmeg
½ teaspoon cinnamon
1 21-ounce can peach pie filling
1 15-ounce can fruit cocktail, drained
1 11-ounce can mandarin oranges, drained
1 8-ounce jar Maraschino cherries, drained
¼ cup crushed pineapple, drained
1 8-ounce carton frozen whipped topping, thawed
1 cup miniature marshmallows
½ cup chopped walnuts

In a large mixing bowl, beat cream cheese until smooth. Add the peach baby food, ginger, nutmeg, and cinnamon. Stir in the pie filling, fruit cocktail, oranges, cherries, and pineapple. Gently add the whipped topping, marshmallows, and nuts. Cover and refrigerate overnight.

Serves six

Orange Fruit Salad

1 20-ounce can pineapple tidbits, drained
1 16-ounce can peach slices, drained
1 11-ounce can mandarin oranges
3 medium bananas, sliced
2 medium apples, peeled, cored, and chopped
1 ¾-ounce package instant vanilla pudding
1½ cups milk
½ cup orange juice
¾ cup sour cream

In a large mixing bowl, combine pineapple, peaches, oranges, bananas, and apples and set aside. In a small bowl, combine pudding mix, milk, and orange juice. Mix with beater on low speed until blended, one or two minutes. Beat in sour cream and then fold into fruit mixture. Cover and refrigerate.

Serves six

Strawberries and Cream

½ quart strawberries, cleaned
1 quart strawberries cleaned, hulled, and halved
¾ cup cold whipping cream
¼ cup honey
1 3-ounce package cream cheese, softened

In a medium-size mixing bowl, combine cream and honey. Using a mixer at high speed, beat cream and honey, until medium-stiff peaks form, then refrigerate. In a small bowl, mix cream cheese and remaining honey. Fold into whipped cream and continue to refrigerate for two hours. Right before serving, add the halved strawberries and gently blend. Pour into individual serving bowls and top with remaining strawberries.

Serves six

Chapter Four

Peace, Comfort, and Main Dishes

While feeling stressed while learning a new job, I asked the Lord to give me confidence. A small, still voice whispered to my heart. It said that I would not be given confidence. What I would get is peace, because out of peace comes confidence.

Confidence comes from knowing who God is and who you are. Quieting my thoughts, I focused on peace. The job became much easier as I relaxed and calmed my thoughts.

Prayer is talking with God, sharing what is in one's heart. As I talked to Him about my situation, I felt a calm assurance and trust. As we learn to trust, our confidence grows in who God is for us. Jesus was a perfect example of asking and receiving. He proclaimed, "Therefore, I say unto you, 'what things so ever ye desire, when ye pray, believe that ye receive them, and ye shall have them'" Mark 11: 24). God hears us when we pray, whether we feel it or not.

God's Word and promises are dependable. They produce stability in our emotions and keep us from being swayed by feelings of uncertainty and insecurity.

Every possible promise is recorded in the Bible. Every possible victory is recorded there as well. It is ours for the taking. Every obstacle and problem experienced is designed to make us become more like Christ. In every situation, God is on our side. He never accuses or condemns. No circumstance, no situation, no person can separate us from God's love.

Romans 8:35–39 states, "Who shall separate us from the love of Christ? Shall tribulation, or distress, or persecution, or famine, or nakedness, or peril, or sword? As it is written, for thy sake we are killed all the daylong; we are accounted as sheep for the slaughter. Nay, in all these things we are more than conquerors through him that loved us. For I am persuaded, that neither death, nor life, nor angels, nor principalities, nor powers, nor things present, nor things to come, nor height, nor depth, nor any other creature, shall be able to separate us from the love of God, which is in Christ Jesus our Lord."

Being confident of God's everlasting love ensures victory is certain. We are more than conquerors because we are secure in God's love. We follow in His footsteps as we face trials, knowing that we will succeed if we hold on to our faith.

Psalm 23 tells us that God has a desire to lead us to green pastures to restore our souls, clean our minds, and heal our hearts. He wants to lead us through pain and fear to peace. While He comforts us, He leads us into righteousness.

Psalm 27:3 states, "Though an host should encamp against me, my heart shall not fear: though war should rise against me, in this will I be confident." John 14:27 tells us, "Peace I leave with you, my peace I give unto you: not as the world gives, give I unto you. Let not your heart be troubled, neither let it be afraid." Life's battles can be brutal. We live in a clash between two kingdoms—the kingdom of God and the kingdom of this world. The world uses fear to keep people from enjoying life. When Jesus walked the earth, He would often tell people, "Do not fear." Learning to rest is a great weapon. We can bring our souls great peace in times of immense pressure. As we learn this, we become transformed. Be encouraged that God will not fail us if we lean on Him. Even if we're temporarily shaken, we will bounce back like a wobble toy coming to alignment with the promises of God.

Our lives can be like a house built upon a rock that stands firm through the storms of life. There may be a whole lot of shaking going on, but we still stand, trusting God through the storms and building unshakable confidence as we work through trials in our lives.

If we see Jesus as our personal Prince of Peace, we will cease to worry. Peace destroys all negativity. It refreshes and energizes us. It enables us to view life in a positive way.

Prayer

Jesus, no matter what happens to me, I can never be lost to your love. Thank you that nothing can keep your love from me. When trouble comes, remind me to run toward you, not away, for that is where I will find peace. Thank you for giving me peace, which produces confidence. I have no need to fear because you are always with me. Amen.

The main course of a meal reminds me of peace. There is a saying, "to keep the main thing, the main thing". The cross of Christ is the main thing in the life of a believer. He is our peace, our anchor. Peace enables us to think clearly and react in a constructive way. Keeping our thoughts and emotions focused on Him is our main thing.

Main Dishes

Beef Oriental

2 tablespoons cooking oil
1 pound sirloin tips, sliced into strips 1¼-inch thick
⅓ cup soy sauce
⅓ cup water
3 tablespoons cornstarch
2 cups 1-inch bias-cut celery slices
2 cups green onions cut into 1-inch pieces
1 green pepper cut in ¼-inch strips
2 5-ounce cans water chestnuts
1 6-ounce can mushrooms
2 cups cooked rice

Add two tablespoons cooking oil to twelve-inch skillet and heat to medium high. Add beef and cook briskly, turning strips over continuously for one or two minutes. In a small bowl, mix together soy sauce, water, and cornstarch. Pour soy sauce mixture over the beef and bring to a boil. Add celery, onions, and green pepper. Cook; stir occasionally, over high heat for about five minutes. Add water chestnuts and mushrooms. Cook two or more minutes or until hot. Serve over cooked rice.

Serves four

Baked Chicken

1 whole baking chicken
2 large potatoes
½ cup peeled carrots
½ teaspoon salt
½ teaspoon pepper
¼ teaspoon garlic powder
¼ teaspoon onion powder

Preheat oven to 325 °F. Rinse chicken and pat dry with paper towels. Place chicken in baking dish with potatoes and carrots arranged around it. Add seasonings. Cover baking dish with lid or foil and bake for two hours. Remove from oven and let it set for 10 minutes. Slice chicken and place on a platter. Place the potatoes and carrots in a separate bowl.

Serves six

Spaghetti and Meatballs

Meatballs:

½ pound ground beef
½ pound sweet Italian sausage
½ pound hot Italian sausage
1 cup bread crumbs
1 teaspoon salt
½ cup oregano
¼ teaspoon pepper
⅛ teaspoon garlic powder
1 egg, beaten
1 tablespoon cooking oil

Sauce:

5 cups canned tomatoes, with juice
2 6-ounce cans tomato paste
1 teaspoon salt
1 teaspoon sugar
1 tablespoon oregano
1 tablespoon basil
2 teaspoons onion powder
2 teaspoons pepper flakes
1 tablespoon parsley

In a large bowl, mix the meatball ingredients together, except the eggs. Add the eggs last. Mix thoroughly. Use a tablespoon to shape mixture into balls. Add one teaspoon cooking oil to a twelve-inch skillet. Heat a skillet to medium high and brown the meatballs.

In a large cooking pot, add the tomatoes, squeezing them to make smaller pieces, and then add the rest of the ingredients. Stir well. Add browned meatballs. Bring to a boil and then lower the heat and simmer 2 hours.

Serves six

Pork Chops and Rice

4 thin-cut pork chops
1 small onion, chopped
2 cloves of garlic, minced
½ cup bell pepper, chopped
½ cup celery, chopped
½ cup green beans, chopped
1 teaspoon salt
½ teaspoon pepper
½ teaspoon garlic powder
½ teaspoon onion powder
3 tablespoons cooking oil
1 cup long grain rice
3 cups hot water, with 2 beef bouillon cubes dissolved

Add one teaspoon cooking oil to a large skillet and heat to medium high. Brown pork chops and cook for about 8 minutes, turning occasionally. Remove pork chops from skillet and add the rest of cooking oil. Add vegetables and seasonings and sauté about 8 minutes. Add water and bring to boil. Add rice and stir well. Return pork chops to the skillet. Bring to a boil and then simmer for 20 minutes.

Serves four

Italian Sausage, Peppers, and Onions

3 cups frozen Potatoes O'Brien
3 links sweet Italian sausage
1 link hot Italian sausage
3 tablespoons olive oil
⅔ of a yellow onion, sliced
⅓ of a red onion, sliced
2 cloves garlic, minced
1 small red bell pepper, chopped
1 green bell pepper, chopped
¾ teaspoon basil
¾ teaspoon oregano
2 tablespoons white wine
2 tablespoons of olive oil

Add two tablespoons olive oil to a large skillet and heat to medium high. Add potatoes and cook for 10 to 15 minutes, stirring occasionally. Pour potatoes into a medium-size bowl and set aside. Place sausage in the same skillet and cook over medium heat until brown on all sides. Remove from skillet and cool and slice them. In the same skillet, add 1 tablespoon of olive oil. Stir in yellow onion, red onion, and garlic and cook 3 minutes. Add the red bell pepper and green bell pepper, basil, and oregano. Stir in white wine. Continue cooking. Stir until peppers and onions are tender. Return sausage slices to skillet with the peppers. Reduce heat to low, cover, and simmer 15 minutes. Add potatoes. Cook 3 minutes longer or until potatoes are heated thoroughly.

Serves six

Pork Chops and Stuffing

Pork Chops:

8 pork chops, sliced thinly
½ teaspoon salt
½ teaspoon pepper
½ teaspoon garlic powder
½ teaspoon onion powder
½ cup tomato juice

Stuffing:

3 tablespoons melted butter
3 cups soft bread crumbs
1 teaspoon salt
¼ teaspoon poultry powder
¼ cup diced celery
¼ cup tomato sauce
2 tablespoons chopped onion
2 tablespoons chopped parsley
Cooking spray

Preheat oven to 350 °F. Mix together the stuffing ingredients and set aside. Wipe chops with a paper towel. Rub with seasonings. Coat a baking pan with cooking spray. Lay 4 pork chops in the cooking pan. Layer the chops with stuffing. Arrange the rest of the pork chops on top. Top with ½ cup tomato juice. Bake for 1 hour.

Serves eight

Hungarian Goulash

2 pounds beef chuck, cut into small cubes
1 cup onions, chopped
1 clove garlic, crushed
2 tablespoons vegetable oil
1 tablespoon enriched flour
1½ teaspoons salt
2 tablespoons paprika
1 8-ounce can tomato sauce
1 16-ounce can tomatoes, drained
One package egg noodles

In a large skillet, brown beef, onion, and garlic until golden. Stir in flour, salt, and paprika. Add remaining ingredients and simmer gently, covered, until meat is tender, about 1½ hours. Prepare noodles according to package directions. Serve goulash over noodles.

Meat Loaf

1½ pounds lean ground beef
1½ pounds lean ground pork
½ cup fine bread crumbs
1 14½-ounce tomato sauce
1 egg, slightly beaten
½ onion, chopped
1 celery stalk, chopped
2 tablespoons chopped parsley
1 tablespoon Worcestershire Sauce
2 teaspoons salt
2 teaspoons pepper

Preheat oven to 350 °F. In a large bowl, mix together all ingredients, reserving ½ cup of tomato sauce. Pack in loaf pan and pour remaining tomato sauce over the top. Bake in the oven for 1 hour. Let stand 15 minutes before serving.

Serves six

Baked Fish

1 whole trout or salmon
2 cups soft bread crumbs
1 teaspoon salt
1 teaspoon pepper
¼ cup parsley
½ teaspoon poultry seasoning
¼ cup melted butter
2 tablespoons lemon juice

Preheat oven to 400 °F. Thoroughly clean fish and place in a well-greased glass pan. Mix together the bread crumbs, salt, chopped parsley, poultry seasoning, pepper, and lemon juice. Stuff fish with bread stuffing and tie with string. Bake 20 minutes.

Serves 4

Beef and Rice

4 cups cooked rice
2½ cups cooked sirloin, cut in thin strips
1 pound fresh button mushrooms
¼ cup butter

Sauce:

3 tablespoons butter
8 ounces fresh white mushrooms, sliced
3 tablespoons flour
1 cup heavy cream
2 cups beef stock
¼ cup tomato paste
¼ cup breadcrumbs
1 cup mozzarella cheese

Preheat oven to 400 °F. Spread rice into the bottom of a greased 9 x 13-inch baking dish. In a preheated large skillet, sauté the mushrooms in butter. Cover rice with beef strips and sautéed mushrooms.

Sauce:

Heat butter in a saucepan. Sauté the mushrooms until tender. Add flour and cook for 2 minutes. Add cream and stock and stir. Reduce heat and simmer until thickened. Whisk in tomato paste.

Pour mushroom sauce over meat mixture. Combine cheese and bread crumbs and sprinkle over sauce. Bake in oven for 25 minutes or until heated completely.

Serves six

Chapter Five

Patience and the Slow Cooker

One of the areas I have needed the most patience in is raising children. Many times I would quickly become angry and expect that anger to result in their good behavior. What I desired was good behavior from my children, but my approach was totally wrong. That method never worked. Flying off the handle was not an effective way to get them to listen to me. Patience had to be practiced constantly. Many fights are the result of short tempers and hasty words. Anger is contrary to the patience God wants to produce in our lives. Patience is too valuable to lose.

Col 1:11 states, "Strengthened with all might, according to his glorious power, unto all patience and longsuffering with joyfulness." James 1:4 states, "But let patience have her perfect work, that ye may be perfect and entire, wanting nothing." Joyfully bearing suffering with patience is quite an achievement. God tells us to be joyful as well as patient in the troubles of life. His grace can support and strengthens us. Trust and patience work together to bring good into all situations. Allow patience to work. It develops while we wait and trust God. When the work of patience is complete in one area, we become whole and complete in that area. Patience strengthens faith and increases wisdom. The purpose of trials is to build us up so we can have a deeper knowledge of God's love and grace in a way we have never known before.

As we learn to live in Christ, we develop the fruit of patience. Patience produces in us completeness, where we learn that God will supply us with everything we need. We need not fear lack. Trials give us the opportunity to develop and possess the qualities of the fruit of the Spirit: love, joy, peace, longsuffering, gentleness, goodness, faithfulness, meekness, and temperance. Every trial brings with it a blessing if we do not give up.

I have to admit, I have days when I lose my patience and feel badly about it. Even though I may have blown it, God does not give up on me. Tomorrow is another day. His mercies are new every morning (Lam. 3:23).

Prayer

Jesus, I ask to be strengthened with all might, according to your glorious power, unto all patience and longsuffering with joy. Help me to keep going no matter what the circumstances are. Let patience bring me to wholeness and joy, and then I will be complete, lacking nothing. Amen.

Crock-Pot or slow cooked food reminds me of patience. Patience gives us the ability to endure waiting without being annoyed or upset. It produces calmness in all situations. Slow cooked meals take several hours to cook. Every ingredient simmers at a low heat until all the flavors are completely combined and fully cooked, ready to be served.

Slow Cooker Recipes

Pork Lo Mein

1 small onion, cut into wedges
2 pounds pork arm steak, trim off fat and cut into 1-inch cubes
1 1-ounce envelope stir-fry seasoning mix
1 8-ounce can sliced water chestnuts
1 8 ounce can sliced bamboo shoots, drained
2 medium stalks celery, sliced
1 pound bag frozen mixed stir-fry vegetables
¼ cup teriyaki baste and glaze
1 pound angel hair pasta cooked according to package directions

Place onion, pork, seasoning mix, water chestnuts, bamboo shoots, and celery in a slow cooker. Cover and cook on low setting 8 to 10 hours or high 4 to 5 hours. Slowly stir in frozen vegetables and teriyaki baste and glaze. Cover and cook another 15 minutes on high or until vegetables are tender. Serve pork mixture over prepared pasta.

Serves eight

Meatball and Gravy Sandwiches

2 medium onions, sliced
2 12-ounce package frozen cooked Swedish-style meatballs
2 12-ounces jars beef gravy
1 teaspoon nutmeg
8 hoagie buns

Place onions in a 4-quart slow cooker. Add meatballs and gravy, combine well. Cover and cook on low heat setting 7 to 8 hours or high 4 to 5 hours. Mix nutmeg into meatball mixture. Cut the hoagie buns horizontally almost in half and place 6 meatballs in each bun. Top with gravy from the slow cooker.

Makes 8 sandwiches

Beef Stew

2 pounds stew meat, cut into cubes
2 tablespoons flour
3 tablespoons vegetable oil
4 carrots, peeled and sliced
6 red potatoes, peeled and cubed
3 celery stalks, cut up
1½ cups cabbage, shredded
1 cup beef broth
1 cup water
1 teaspoon salt
1 teaspoon pepper
1 teaspoon garlic powder
1 teaspoon onion powder
1 teaspoon fine herbs
1 small can peas, drained

Pour vegetable oil into a large skillet and heat to medium high. On a plate, sprinkle meat with flour. Brown the meat in the hot skillet for about 10 minutes. Remove meat from skillet and then place all the ingredients, except the peas, in the slow cooker. Stir and cover the pot. Cook on low setting 8 to 10 hours or high 4 to 5 hours. At the last ½ hour add the peas.

Serves six

Bread Pudding

3 slices bread, cut into cubes
1 tablespoon butter, melted
½ cup brown sugar
¼ teaspoon salt
½ teaspoon cinnamon
2 eggs, lightly beaten
2 cups hot milk
½ teaspoon vanilla
½ cup seedless raisins
½ cup chopped nuts (optional)
4 cups water
2 ounces jar caramel sauce

In a large mixing bowl, mix all ingredients together except water and caramel sauce. Place mixture in a buttered mold that you can fit inside the slow cooker. Cover the container with aluminum foil. Pour water into slow cooker and place the foil-covered mold in the pot. Cover the pot and cook on low 5 hours or on high 2 ½ hours. Remove from slow cooker. Drizzle caramel sauce while warm.

Serves four

Western–Style Bean Bake

2 tablespoons cooking oil
1 pound smoked sausage, sliced thin
2 cloves garlic, minced
½ cup onion, chopped
½ cup green pepper, chopped
3 15-ounce cans of baked beans, drained
1 8-ounce can tomato sauce
1 2-ounce can sliced black olives
⅓ cup barbecue sauce
1 cup sour cream
½ teaspoon salt
½ teaspoon pepper
½ teaspoon garlic powder
½ teaspoon onion powder

In a large preheated skillet, add oil and then combine sausage, garlic, onion, and bell pepper. Cook over medium heat, stirring frequently, until sausage is browned, about 8 minutes. Drain.

In a slow cooker, combine meat mixture, baked beans, black olives, tomato sauce, barbecue sauce, sour cream, salt, pepper, garlic powder, and onion powder. Stir well. Cover and cook on low 5 hours or high 2 ½ hours.

Serves six

Taco Short Ribs

4 pounds short ribs
1 package taco seasoning mix
1 10½-ounce can beef consommé
1 green pepper, diced
1 small onion, sliced

Brown the meat in a preheated skillet and then drain off excess fat. In a bowl, mix the taco seasoning and consommé. Add green pepper and onion to the bowl. Put short ribs in slow cooker and pour sauce into pot. Cover the pot and cook on low 6 to 8 hours or high 3 to 4 hours. Serves six

Sausage, Vegetable, and Noodle Soup

½ pound kielbasa sausage, cut into ½-inch slices
1 8-ounce can tomato sauce
1 16-ounce can stewed tomatoes
1 package onion soup mix
1 cup water
1 10-ounce package frozen mixed vegetables, partially thawed
½ cup uncooked 1-inch pieces of noodles

In a hot skillet, brown the sausage for about 5 minutes per side. Put meat, tomato sauce, stewed tomatoes, soup mix, and water into slow cooker. Cover the pot and cook on low 6 to 8 hours or high 3 to 4 hours. Add the frozen vegetables and noodle pieces. Cover pot and cook on high 30 minutes.

Serves four

Noodles with Spinach

2 10-ounce packages frozen spinach, thawed
1 cup shredded cheddar cheese
1 10ounce can cream of mushroom soup
½ cup onion, chopped
⅛ teaspoon nutmeg
¼ cup butter
2 cups cooked noodles

In a large mixing bowl, combine all ingredients and stir well. Place mixture in slow cooker and cook on low 4 to 5 hours or high 3 hours. Stir several times during cooking. Serve over noodles.

Serves four

Spinach and Cheese

2 10-ounce packages frozen spinach, thawed and drained
2 cups cottage cheese, cream–style or small curd
½ cup butter, cut into small pieces
1½ cups cheddar cheese, shredded
3 eggs, beaten
¼ cup flour
1 teaspoon salt

In a large mixing bowl, combine all ingredients well. Grease the slow cooker with butter. Place the ingredients inside, cover, and cook on high for 1 hour, and then on low 4 to 6 hours.

Serves four

Carrots and Cheese

2 pounds carrots, peeled, cut into ½-inch slices
1 medium onion, sliced
1 teaspoon salt
¾ cup water
3 tablespoons honey
4 tablespoons butter
1 cup cheddar cheese, grated
½ cup bread crumbs
2 tablespoons flour

Place carrots, onions, salt, and ¼ cup water in slow cooker. Cover the pot and cook on low for 8 to 10 hours or high for 4 to 5 hours. About 45 minutes before serving, mix the remaining water and flour to a thick paste, and then pour over the vegetables in slow cooker. Add the honey and stir thoroughly. Add cheese and dots of butter. Cover the pot and cook on high for 15 minutes, until cheese melts. Stir contents in pot well. Sprinkle top of vegetables with bread crumbs. Cover the pot and cook on low an additional 30 minutes.

Serves six

Chapter 6

Gentleness and Casseroles

always remember having a strong sense of responsibility. I felt responsible for the behavior of my younger two brothers as well as keeping the house in order. All my hard work was futile. My brothers didn't mind me, and the house was always a mess. As a result I felt frustrated and burdened. It wasn't until I was a young adult and read Matthew 11:30 that I started to understand that I was carrying unnecessary and uncomfortable burdens. Jesus eases the pressure and heaviness of life as we are taught and trained by Him. He carries our burdens for us.

Matthew 11:28–30 states, "Come unto me, all ye that labor and are heavy laden, and I will give you rest. Take my yoke upon you, and learn of me; for I am meek and lowly in heart and ye shall find rest unto your souls, for my yoke is easy, and my burden is light." A yoke is a heavy wooden harness that fits over the shoulders of a pair of oxen as they pull heavy loads or plow the ground. It helps the animals work in unison, distributing the weight between them. Sometimes a younger, inexperienced ox is yoked to an older, experienced one. As they work the field, the younger one is mentored by the older one.

The world gives us a yoke of trouble, worry, hurts, and weariness. Sin, shame, and guilt are an intense burden to carry. Jesus tells us to shed that old yoke and be yoked with Him. His yoke is lined with love and fits comfortably. When we find His grace, life becomes manageable. He came to free us from life's weighty cares.

Christ's yoke is light and redeems us with forgiveness and grace. Jesus is always inviting us to come into His presence where we are able to lay down our worries and cares. Gentleness produces rest and peace. It guards against negative mindsets, anger, anxiety, strife, and bitterness. Peace can flourish in a gentle person. A soft and gentle answer can disarm a furious person. It weakens resentments and arguments.

Prayer

Jesus, I come to you, where I find rest for my soul. In your caring presence, I find refuge. I lay down all my heavy burdens, anxieties and cares and take up your yoke of peace and gentleness. Thank you for being meek and lowly. Teach me to be the same. Amen.

Casseroles remind me of gentleness. Gentle people are easy to be around. They have a calming effect on others, which decreases tension and results in less stress for everyone. Casseroles are easy to prepare and convenient to serve.

Casseroles

Hamburger Bean Casserole

1 pound ground beef
1 cup onions, chopped
2 cloves garlic
1 tablespoon prepared mustard
1 1-ounce can pork and beans
1 8-ounce can tomato sauce
Dash of garlic powder, salt, and pepper

Drop Biscuits:

3 cups flour
1 teaspoon salt
1 tablespoon sugar
4 teaspoons baking powder
1 teaspoon baking soda
4 tablespoons butter, softened
2 eggs, lightly beaten
1½ cups buttermilk

Preheat oven to 350 °F. In a medium-size frying pan, sauté ground beef, onion, and garlic. Stir in mustard, pork and beans, tomato sauce, and spices. Pour into a casserole dish. Now prepare the biscuits.

Mix together flour, salt, sugar, baking powder, and baking soda. Cut butter into the dry ingredients until mixture is textured like cornmeal. In a separate bowl, mix the eggs with buttermilk and then stir into dry mixture. Mix just enough to make uniformly moistened dough.

Drop by the spoonful on top of casserole dish. Bake for 20 minutes or until bubbly. Take out of the oven and let set for 15 minutes before serving.

Serves six

Green Chile Chicken Casserole

⅔ cup chicken broth
1 cup canned chopped green chilies, drained
½ cup onion, chopped
½ cup sour cream
½ teaspoon salt
½ teaspoon ground cumin
½ teaspoon black pepper
5 ounces condensed cream of chicken soup, undiluted
5 ounces condensed cream of celery soup, undiluted
1 clove garlic
Cooking spray
12 6-inch corn tortillas
2 cups shredded cooked chicken
1 tablespoon chili powder
1 cup finely shredded sharp cheddar cheese

Preheat oven to 350 °F. In a large saucepan, whisk together chicken broth, green chilies, onion, sour cream, salt, cumin, pepper, cream of chicken soup, cream of celery soup, and garlic. Stir constantly until it reaches a boil and then remove from heat. Coat a casserole dish with oil. Spread in ½ cup of soup mixture. Sprinkle ½ tablespoon chili powder over the top. Arrange 6 tortillas over the soup mixture and top with ½ cup chicken and ¼ cup cheese. Repeat layers. Spread remaining soup mixture over cheese. Bake 30 minutes or until bubbly.

Serves six

Country Breakfast Casserole

1 12-ounce roll breakfast sausage
2 cups shredded cheddar cheese
6 eggs, beaten
1 cup water
½ cup milk
1 package country gravy mix
6 slices bread, cut into 1-inch cubes
2 tablespoons melted butter
1 tablespoon paprika

Preheat oven to 325 °F. Cook crumbled sausage in a medium frying pan. Cook over medium heat until brown, stirring occasionally. Drain off grease. Spread in a lightly greased 8 x 11-inch baking dish. Spread cheese over sausage.

Beat eggs, water, milk, and gravy mix in medium bowl. Whisk until well blended. Pour over cheese. Arrange bread evenly over mixture. Drizzle butter over bread and sprinkle with paprika. Bake uncovered 40 minutes or until knife inserted comes out clean.
Serves four

Cheese, Broccoli, and Tuna Bake

Cheese Sauce:

3 tablespoons butter
3 tablespoons flour
½ teaspoon salt
⅛ teaspoon ground black or white pepper1
½ cups milk
1 cup grated sharp Cheddar

Melt butter; remove from heat. Stir in flour, salt and pepper. Gradually add milk, stirring until well mixed. Cook over low heat, stirring constantly, until thickened and smooth. Cook for 5 minutes longer; add cheese. Stir until smooth and well blended. Set aside.

1 12-ounce package frozen egg noodles or packaged egg noodles
1 1- ounce can condensed cheddar cheese soup
1 5-ounce can evaporated milk
1 teaspoon minced onions
2 celery stalks, chopped finely
1 12-ounce can albacore tuna, drained
1 4-ounce can mushroom pieces, drained
1 10-ounce package chopped broccoli, thawed
1 cup shredded medium cheddar cheese

Preheat oven to 350 °F. Cook noodles according to package directions. Drain. In a medium saucepan, blend soup and milk into a smooth sauce. Add onions, mushrooms, celery, and tuna. Cook over medium heat until it boils. Simmer 10 minutes, and then remove from heat and set aside. Layer half noodles, half tuna mixture, half broccoli, and half cheese sauce in a casserole dish. Repeat layers. Bake 20 minutes. Then add cheese and bake 15 more minutes.

Serves six

Eggplant, Zucchini, Mushroom Casserole

1 large eggplant, peeled and sliced into ¼-inch slices
2 large zucchinis, peeled and sliced into ¼-inch slices
1 cup mushrooms, sliced
1 clove garlic, minced
1 15-ounce can tomato sauce
1 6-ounce can tomato paste
½ teaspoon salt
½ teaspoon pepper
¼ teaspoon garlic powder
¼ teaspoon onion powder
1 cup shredded mozzarella cheese

Preheat oven to 350 °F. In a casserole dish, layer eggplant, zucchini, and mushrooms. In a medium bowl, mix tomato sauce, tomato paste, garlic, and seasonings. Pour over vegetables. Bake 30 minutes. Add cheese and bake 15 more minutes.

Serves six

Easy One-Dish Chicken and Rice Bake

1 10-ounce can cream of celery soup
1 cup water
½ cup celery, chopped
¾ cup uncooked long-grain white rice
½ teaspoon paprika
¼ teaspoon pepper
4 boneless chicken breast halves

Preheat oven to 375 °F. Mix soup, water, rice, paprika, and pepper in a shallow 2-quart baking dish. Top with chicken and season with additional paprika and pepper. Cover and bake for 45 minutes or until done.

For a little extra kick, add 2 tablespoons melted butter and 2 tablespoons Red Hot sauce to the soup mixture.

Serves four

Ground Beef Casserole

1 pound ground beef
1 small onion, diced
1 package Sloppy Joe mix
1 tablespoon cumin
1 6-ounce can tomato paste
1¼ cup water
2 cups elbow macaroni
1 15-ounce can corn, drained
2 cups mild or medium cheddar cheese, grated

Preheat oven to 350 °F. In an eight-inch saucepan, cook beef and onions, stirring constantly until it loses the red color. Stir in Sloppy Joe mix followed by tomato paste and water. Bring to a boil. Reduce heat and simmer 10 minutes.

Meanwhile, cook macaroni according to package directions. Stir in meat mixture, corn, and 1 cup cheese. Turn into a greased 2-quart casserole dish. Sprinkle with the rest of the cheese. Bake uncovered for 45 minutes.

Serves six

Chinese Green Bean Casserole

1 quart green beans cut into 1 or 2-inch pieces
1 10-ounce can condensed cream of celery soup
½ cup celery, diagonally sliced
1 3-ounce can slice mushroom
1 8½-ounce can water chestnuts, sliced and drained
1 tablespoon soy sauce
1 4-ounce can pimentos, drained, chopped
¾ cup chow mien noodles

Preheat oven to 375 °F. Bring a pan of water to a boil and add green beans. Cook for 5minutes. Drain water from beans. Place beans into a casserole dish. In a medium bowl, combine cream of celery soup, celery, mushrooms, water chestnuts, soy sauce, and pimentos and pour over green beans. Bake 45 minutes. Remove from oven and stir gently. Top with noodles and bake for 10 minutes or until tender.

Serves six

Wild Rice with Mushroom and Almonds

1 box of wild rice
1 small package sliced almonds
1 8-ounce can sliced mushrooms and stems, drained
2 tablespoons chopped chives or green onions
1 ½ cups chicken broth

Cook rice according directions on the box. Add almonds, mushrooms, and chives and mix well. Set aside and let cool completely. Pour the broth into a cooking pan and bring to a boil. Put the mixture into a 1½-quart casserole dish. Pour the chicken broth over the mixture and stir well. Cover and bake for 1 hour.

Serves four

Tamale Pie

3 bacon slices, diced
1 large onion, chopped
1 small green pepper, chopped
2 cloves garlic, minced
1½ pounds ground beef
2 teaspoons salt
½ teaspoon pepper
1 small package chili seasoning
2 tablespoons chili powder
1 12-ounce can whole kernel corn, drained
2 4-ounce can chopped black olives, drained
1 10-ounce can tomato soup
1 1-pound can diced tomatoes
1 package (6 ounces) cornbread mix
½ cup Mexican cheese, grated

Preheat oven to 375 °F. Fry bacon until crisp and then drain off all but 2 tablespoons fat. Add onion, green pepper, and garlic, and sauté until tender. Add meat and brown. Add salt, pepper, chili seasonging, chili powder, corn, olives, tomato soup, and tomatoes. Mix well and simmer for 15 minutes. Pour mixture into a greased 12 x 8-inch baking dish. Mix cornbread according to directions on the package. Spread over meat mixture. Sprinkle with cheese and bake for 35 minutes.

Serves six

Chapter Seven

Goodness and Gifts of Food

While I was recuperating from an illness, a friend brought over a meal. What a relief it was to my family and me. My family was happy that they did not have to eat takeout food again or prepare a meal. I will always remember the heartfelt comfort and support I felt from my friend. Thinking about it still reminds me how appreciated her gift was.

Psalm 34:8 states, "O taste and see that the LORD is good: blessed is the man that trusteth in him." Here is a warm invitation to test God's goodness. Its evidence is all around us; all we have to do is purposely upgrade our attitude and become aware, in a fresh new way that God is kind. We often wish we could escape our problems, but problems are designed to lead us deeper into God's kindness.

He showers mercy on those who trust Him and look to Him in all situations. Revering and showing respect and honor to God helps us see that God is active in our lives and working on our behalf. He is cheerfully inclined to prove Himself to us.

Relationships require that we must actively participate. Filling our thoughts with the Word of God, meditating on His character, and having heartfelt communication with Him positions us to know what He is really like. The more familiar we are with Him, the better we know Him. Taking steps to know God will prove time and time again that He is good and kind.

By letting God's goodness touch your heart, that goodness will spill over onto others. He desires to give us blessing upon blessing.

Prayer

Jesus, I answer your invitation to taste and see that you are good. Reveal your goodness to me, I want to experience it. Show me opportunities where I can be generous to share with others. Amen.

Gifts of food, remind me of the fruit of the Spirit—goodness. Being kind to others can bring encouragement, comfort, and healing to the emotions and body. It feels good to give. It is more blessed to give than to receive.

Recipes for Gifts of Food

Marinated Vegetables

¼ cup vinegar
¼ cup vegetable oil
1 tablespoon sugar
1 teaspoon salt
½ teaspoon oregano or thyme leaves
½ teaspoon dill weed
½ teaspoon seasoned salt
⅛ teaspoon pepper
4 cups assorted vegetables, such as cauliflower, carrots, mushrooms, cherry tomatoes, broccoli flowerets, zucchini, onion, cucumber

Place vegetables in a 1½ quart jar. In a small bowl, combine remaining ingredients. Mix well and pour over vegetables. Cover and refrigerate for 6 hours or overnight. Shake covered jar occasionally.

Granola

3½ cups oat meal
½ cup sunflower seeds
½ cup raisins
½ cup coconut
¼ cup whole wheat flour
¼ cup soy flour
¼ cup cornmeal
½ teaspoon salt
½ cup nut meal
½ cup wheat germ
½ cup white flour
¼ cup hot water
½ cup honey or brown sugar
¼ cup vegetable oil

Preheat oven to 250 °F. In a large mixing bowl, combine oats, sunflower seeds, raisins, coconut, whole wheat flour, soy flour, cornmeal, salt, nut meal, wheat germ, and white flour. Add water, honey, and oil. Mix well. Cover two large baking sheets with mixture. Bake 45 minutes or until crisp. Stir every 15 minutes.

Apple Butter

4 pounds cooking apples (Granny Smith or Gravenstein), peeled, cored, and chopped
1 cup apple cider
2 cups sugar
½ teaspoon salt
2 teaspoons cinnamon
½ teaspoon ground cloves
½ teaspoon allspice
1 lemon, grated rind and juice

Place apples in a large pot and add apple cider. Cook 20 minutes, until apples are soft. Add sugar, salt, cinnamon, cloves, allspice, and lemon. Continue to cook over low heat, stirring frequently to prevent sticking, until mixture is thick, about 2 hours. Cool 1 to 2 hours.
Makes three pints

Cheese Ball

1 16-ounce package of cream cheese, softened to room temperature
1 small jar Old English cheese
1 small triangle Roquefort cheese
½ teaspoon instant onion (or more to taste)

Mix all the ingredients together. Roll into two balls. Refrigerate until firm. Roll in parsley or nuts. Serve with crackers.

Amish Friendship Bread

Day 1: Combine 1 cup flour, 1 cup sugar, and 1 cup milk in a zip-lock bag. Mush well. Do not refrigerate.

Day 2: Mash the bag, with your hands

Day 3: Mash the bag

Day 4: Mash the bag

Day 5: Mash the bag

Day 6: Add 1 cup flour, 1 cup sugar, and 1 cup milk to the bag. Mash well, pour 4 one-cup starters into 4 large zip-lock bags, and give to four friends along with the following instructions.

With the remaining batter, put in a large bowl and combine with:

1 cup oil

½ cup milk

3 eggs

1 teaspoon vanilla

In a separate bowl, mix:

2 cups flour

1 teaspoon salt

1 large vanilla pudding mix

1 cup chopped nuts

½ teaspoon baking soda

1 cup sugar

1½ teaspoon baking powder

2 teaspoons cinnamon

Add the dry ingredients to the wet ingredients and mix thoroughly. Put into two greased loaf pans that have been coated with sugar and cinnamon. Add dried fruit if desired. Bake at 325 °F for one hour.

Give the bread to a friend along with a bag of batter and the recipe.

Raisin Rice Pudding

2 cups cooked rice
3 eggs, well beaten
4 cups milk
½ cup granulated sugar
¼ teaspoon salt
1 teaspoon nutmeg or cinnamon
1 cup seedless raisins

Preheat oven to 350 °F. Mix together all ingredients in the order given. Blend well and pour into a buttered 2-quart baking dish. Bake for 1½ hours, stirring pudding halfway through. Remove from oven, cool and serve chilled.

Double Topping Apple Pie

1 pie shell, defrosted to room temperature
1 21-ounce can apple pie filling

Topping One/Cream Cheese:

4 ounces cream cheese
¼ cup sugar

Topping Two/Crisp Topping:

½ cup rolled oats
⅓ cup all-purpose flour
⅓ cup firmly packed brown sugar
½ cup butter

Preheat oven to 350 °F. Pour apple pie filling into the pie shell. In a small bowl, mix the cream cheese and sugar at low speed. In another small bowl, mix together the rolled oats, flour, and brown sugar. Add butter. Spoon teaspoons of the cream cheese topping onto the apple pie filling, leaving space between the teaspoons of cream cheese, and then drizzle the crisp topping between the cream cheese topping, filling all the open spaces. Bake for 40 to 45 minutes.

Granola Bars

½ cup brown sugar
½ cup light corn syrup
½ cup peanut butter
½ cup peanuts
3 ½ cups granola

Butter a 9-inch square pan. In a large saucepan, combine corn syrup and brown sugar. Stir constantly over medium heat stirring until it comes to a boil. Remove pan from the heat and stir in peanut butter until well blended. Stir in granola and peanuts until thoroughly coated. Press into the square pan. Cool and cut.

Zucchini Bread

3 eggs
2¼ cups sugar
3 teaspoons vegetable oil
2 cups zucchini, grated
3 cups flour
¼ teaspoon baking powder
1 teaspoon salt
1 teaspoon baking soda
3 teaspoons cinnamon
1 cup chopped nuts (optional)

Preheat oven 350 °F. Beat eggs until light and fluffy. Add sugar and oil. Blend well. Stir in zucchini. Sift in flour, baking powder, salt, soda, and cinnamon and blend with cream mixture. Fold in chopped nuts and pour into greased and floured bread pan. Bake for 1 hour.

Salsa

3 quarts diced tomatoes, drained
2 cans green chili
½ cup lemon juice
1 medium onion, finely chopped
1 clove garlic, crushed
¼ teaspoon black pepper
1 teaspoon oregano
¼ cup dried parsley
Louisiana Hot Sauce to taste

Mix all ingredients together and let set for at least 3 hours. Pour into a jar. Bring salsa and a bag of tortilla chips to a friend.

Chapter Eight

Faithfulness and Family Recipes

As a new believer in Christ, I made a commitment to set aside at least fifteen minutes each day to pray, meditate, and read the Bible. That was a starting point. Modern life is very busy. Finding quiet time can be very difficult, but it is well worth it. Communication with God is the basis of spiritual life. It keeps faith alive.

Building my life on a foundation of prayer and reading God's Word, I had peace and strength when diagnosed with breast cancer. Through the trials of life, I have learned to trust Him. When I told my husband the news, I said, "I have strong faith. I know that I am going to be all right." The confidence and assurance I had amazed even me. I was mindful to build my inner life on God and His word, and He proved His faithfulness to me.

Proverbs 28:20 states, "A faithful man will abound with blessings." God's word is like a road map. It directs us to contentment. Faithfulness, commitment, and dependability bring us stability, strength, and life. Just like consistent daily exercise transforms our bodies and builds muscle, spending time each day in God's presence results in righteousness, peace, and joy

Psalm 117: 1–2 states, "Praise the Lord, all you nations; extol him, all you peoples. For great is his love toward us, and the faithfulness of the Lord endures forever. Praise the Lord." Psalm 117 is the shortest chapter in the Bible, yet it speaks volumes. Every person in the world—male, female, rich, poor, every ethnic group and nationality—is equally loved by God. The Bible makes it clear that He created all people, and He loves all people. His love is unlimited. Being faithful to all, His blessings are extended to those who are faithful to Him, regardless of their position in life.

The most quoted verse of the New Testament is John 3:16, "For God so loved the world, that he gave his only begotten Son, that whosoever believeth in him should not perish, but have everlasting life."

His grace and mercy are free to all because of the redemptive work of Jesus, the Messiah. He is seeking people who are committed to Him so he can help and strengthen them.

Faithfulness is what drives our behavior. We are faithful to what we are committed to. It is the core of who we are. We can be committed to a life of selfishness or a life of righteousness. Faithfulness is about our relationship to God and others. Jesus said the greatest commandment is to love God and others. Christianity is based on relationship, not performance. As we walk with Christ and learn who He is, we take on more of His nature, or the fruit of the Spirit, into our hearts, minds, words, and actions. Faithfulness keeps us on a steady course and keeps us from compromising our beliefs.

Prayer

Jesus, let love and faithfulness never leave me. Bind them around my neck and write them on the tablet of my heart. I desire to be true to what you teach. Amen (Prov. 3:3).

Heritage foods, or those old family recipes that have been passed down to generations, remind me of faithfulness. They are tried, true, and trusted. Likewise, God is faithful throughout the generations, and His promises are trustworthy. His Word is tried, true, and trusted as well.

Family Recipes

Great-Grandpa's Favorite Oatmeal Cookies

¾ cup shortening or butter
1 cup sugar
2 eggs
1 cup plus 2 tablespoons flour
1 teaspoon baking powder
¼ teaspoon salt
1 teaspoon cinnamon
⅓ cup milk
1 teaspoon vanilla
1 cup seedless raisins
3 cups oats

Preheat oven to 350 °F. In a large mixing bowl, cream sugar and shortening (or butter) together with an electric beater. Next, beat in eggs one at a time. In a separate bowl, sift together flour, baking powder, salt, and cinnamon and then add to creamed mixture, alternating with milk. Mix in vanilla, raisins, and oats. Drop onto baking sheet and bake for 10 to 12 minutes. Makes 24 cookies

Granny's Dressing

½ quart mayonnaise
1 pint buttermilk
1 teaspoon minced onion
1 teaspoon garlic salt
½ teaspoon onion salt
1 teaspoon favorite all purpose seasoning.

Mix all ingredients well. Pour into serving bottle and refrigerate before serving.
Makes 1 ½ quarts

Uncle Mike's Chile

2 pounds ground lean beef
1 tablespoon Olive oil
1 onion, chopped
2 cloves garlic, minced
1 green pepper, chopped
1 15-ounce kidney beans, undrained
1 15-ounce can pinto beans, undrained
1 15-ounce can stewed tomatoes, undrained
1 15-ounce can tomato sauce
1 6-ounce can tomato paste
2 teaspoons cumin
1 tablespoon chili powder (or more to taste)
1 1-ounce package prepared chili seasoning
½ teaspoon garlic powder
½ teaspoon onion powder
½ teaspoon salt
1 teaspoon black pepper

In a large skillet, brown ground beef and drain. In a large pot, heat olive oil. Sauté onions, garlic, and green pepper until softened. Add the meat, kidney beans, pinto beans, stewed tomatoes, tomato sauce, and tomato paste to the pot. Stir in cumin, chili powder, chili seasoning, garlic powder, onion powder, salt, and pepper. Bring to boil. Reduce heat to low and simmer about 3 hours, stirring every 15 minutes or so.

Serves six

Dad's Stuffed Cabbage Rolls

*1½ pounds lean ground beef
½ pound Italian sweet sausage
1 medium onion
2 clove garlic, minced
2 cups cooked rice
1 tablespoon salt
1 tablespoon pepper
1 teaspoon garlic powder
1 teaspoon onion powder
1 tablespoon paprika
1 large head cabbage
2 cups of water (or enough to cover the cabbage placed in a kettle)
1 14-ounce can tomato sauce

Cook rice according to directions on the box and set aside. Place a large skillet on high heat and cook the beef, sausage, onion, and garlic. Cook until meat is done. Add cooked rice, salt, pepper, garlic powder, onion powder, and paprika and set aside. In a large kettle, add enough water to steam cabbage leaves. Bring water to a boil. Put cabbage in boiling water and cook until the cabbage is soft, about 5 minutes. Remove cabbage and drain. After the cabbage has cooled down, pull leaves off and set on a plate.

Put about 2 to 3 tablespoons of meat mixture in each cabbage leave and make into a roll. Place each roll seam-side down in a dutch oven. Cover rolls with tomato sauce. Bring to a boil, cover, and simmer for one hour.

Serves six
* If you like it spicier, use ½ pound less ground beef and ½ pound hot Italian sausage

Uma's Pot Roast

5 pounds beef chuck
1 tablespoon paprika
½ teaspoon salt
½ teaspoon pepper
½ teaspoon garlic powder
½ teaspoon onion powder
3 tablespoons olive oil
3 bell peppers, sliced
2 onions, chopped
1 carrot, sliced
3 cloves garlic
1 cup red wine or beef stock
1 8-ounce can tomato sauce
2 tablespoons red wine vinegar
½ teaspoon sugar
½ teaspoon pepper
1 teaspoon dried marjoram

Preheat oven to 300 °F. Heat olive oil in a large skillet over medium-high heat. Sprinkle roast with paprika, ½ teaspoon salt, ½ teaspoon pepper, garlic powder, and onion powder. Brown the roast for about 15 minutes on each side. Place in a large ovenproof casserole dish or dutch oven. Add bell peppers, onion, carrots, and garlic.

In the same skillet, add wine, vinegar, tomato sauce, and sugar, scraping to loosen any brown bits. Add remaining pepper and marjoram. Pour over meat and vegetables and cover. Bake in the oven for 4 to 5 hours. Remove from oven when meat is tender. Cover with foil to keep it warm. Remove vegetables with a slotted spoon. Place in a medium bowl and use a potato masher to make puree. To make gravy, place puree in a saucepan, add meat juices and drippings, and cook over medium heat until thickened, adding seasoning to flavor. Cook about 10 to 15 minutes. Slice roast and spoon gravy over it.

Serves eight

Grandpa's Old-Fashioned Butter Beans

2 cups dried lima or butter beans
5 cups water
1 medium onion, chopped
1½ teaspoon light brown sugar
½ teaspoon salt
¼ teaspoon pepper
1 medium ham hock

Sort the beans, removing unwanted ones. Wash in a colander under running water. Presoak the beans in a large mixing bowl with enough water to cover them overnight. Just before cooking, drain the water from the beans and rinse again. Place beans in a dutch oven and add six cups of water. Next, add onions, brown sugar, salt, pepper, and the ham hock to the pot. Bring water to a boil and then reduce heat to a simmer. Cover the dutch oven and cook two hours. Remove ham.

Serves six

Mama's Macaroni and Cheese

1 pound macaroni, cooked according to package directions
2 tablespoons butter
2 tablespoons flour
2 egg yolks, beaten
1 cup milk
1 cup chicken stock
8 ounces cream cheese, softened
1 cup shredded cheddar cheese
1 cup shredded Monterey Jack cheese
Salt and pepper to taste
½ cup cheddar cheese
½ cup pale cheddar cheese

Preheat oven to 350 °F. In an 8-inch pan, melt butter. Slowly stir in flour and heat until thickened. In a medium mixing bowl, combine egg yolks, milk, and chicken stock and whisk until thickened. Add cream cheese to milk mixture and whisk until well blended. Bring to a boil and then turn to low heat. Add shredded cheddar and Monterey Jack cheeses. Mix the macaroni with the cheese sauce. Season the mixture with salt and pepper. Pour the macaroni and cheese into a 12-inch baking dish. Top the dish with cheddar cheese and pale cheddar cheese. Bake in the oven for 35 minutes or until macaroni and cheese start to bubble.

Serves six

Aunt Mary's Boston Baked Beans

1 pound dried navy beans
1 medium onion, diced
½ cup molasses
½ teaspoon dried mustard
½ cup firmly packed brown sugar
1 teaspoon salt
¼ pound lean salt pork, diced

Sort beans and wash thoroughly in a colander under cold water. Place the beans in a large mixing bowl with enough water to cover them. Soak overnight. Drain and place the beans and onions in a 12-inch pot. Add water to cover. Bring to a boil, cover, and then simmer 1 hour. Drain the liquid into a small bowl.

Measure 1 cup of the bean liquid and combine the molasses, mustard, brown sugar, and salt in a medium mixing bowl. Place half the pork and all of the beans into a baking dish. Pour molasses mixture over top. Add just enough saved liquid to cover beans. Top with remaining salt pork, pressing down into liquid, and then cover.

Bake for 4 hours. After 2 hours, check beans and if dry, add more of the saved liquid to keep them moist. After 4 hours, uncover and bake 1 hour longer or until beans are deep brown and tender.

Serves six

Aunt Janean's Herb-Roasted Chicken

1 roasting chicken (about 4 pounds)
1 6-ounce package of herb bread stuffing
1 cup of hot water with one chicken bouillon cube dissolved
3 tablespoons butter
1 large onion
2 cloves garlic
¾ cups frozen spinach, chopped, thawed, and squeezed of water
2 ounces baked ham, cubed
½ teaspoon dried rosemary
½ teaspoon dried sage
¼ cup heavy cream
2 tablespoons lemon juice
1 tablespoon poultry seasoning

Preheat oven to 350 °F. Rinse chicken and pat dry with paper towels. Place chicken in baking dish. In a large mixing bowl, toss stuffing with bouillon water. Melt butter in a large skillet over medium heat and then add garlic and onion. After sautéing 5 minutes, add spinach, ham, rosemary, and sage. Sauté for another 2 minutes. Add spinach mixture to stuffing. In a small mixing bowl, combine the heavy cream and lemon juice. Add to spinach mixture, combining well. Spoon the stuffing loosely into chicken cavity until three-quarters full. Fold skin over openings and close with a skewer. Tuck wings under chicken. Sprinkle outside of chicken with poultry seasoning. Roast chicken for about 1 hour and 45 minutes or until temperature reaches 180 °F.

Serves four

Uncle Steve's Scallops and Mashed Potatoes

5 pounds Yukon Gold Potatoes, peeled and quartered
8 ounces cream cheese, softened
1 cup sour cream
Salt and pepper to salt
¼ cup butter, softened
½ cup milk
Zest from one small lemon
2 tablespoons lemon juice
1 pound cooked scallops, or as much as you desire

Place potatoes in a large saucepan and cover with water. Add a little salt and bring water to a boil over medium heat. Cook until tender but still firm and drain. In a large mixing bowl, combine potatoes, cream cheese, butter, salt, pepper, and milk. Use a potato masher to mash until smooth. Stir in the lemon zest, lemon juice and scallops.

Serves four

Uncle Jim's Chopped Suey

2 tablespoons vegetable oil
2 cloves garlic, minced
8 carrots, sliced diagonally
2 cups green beans, cut into 2-inch pieces
1 large cabbage, shredded
2 bunches bok choy
1 cup soy sauce
1 bunch celery, sliced diagonally
1 bunch green onions, chopped
3½ pounds bean sprouts
4 large bell peppers
3 cups cooked rice, cooked according to package directions

In a large, hot stir-fry pan, add oil, garlic, and carrots and cook for 8 minutes, stirring constantly. Add green beans and cook 5 more minutes, stirring occasionally. Add the cabbage and bok choy and cook for additional 5 minutes. Add soy sauce, celery, onions, bean sprouts, and bell pepper and continue cooking, stirring constantly, for 15 minutes, until the vegetables are tender yet crisp. Serve over rice.

Serves six

Grandma Celine's Granmere

1½ cup flour
3 teaspoons baking powder
Dash of salt
2 eggs, beaten
¾ cup milk
16 ounces maple syrup
12 ounces water

In a medium size mixing bowl, sift the flour, baking powder, and salt. Mix in the eggs and milk. Let it rise 15 minutes.

In a large cooking pot, mix the maple syrup and water over high heat and bring to boil. Drop the flour mixture by tablespoons, like dumplings, into the boiling water. Cover and cook for 15 minutes at medium heat, without looking in the pot. Remove dumplings onto a bowl. Enjoy—it is sweet

Serves four

Chapter Nine

Meekness and Soup

At age twelve, I started cooking because I enjoyed it. One of the dishes I used to prepare was broiled chicken. I just put a little salt and pepper on chicken pieces and broiled it in the oven. My dad would eat it and say how delicious it was. I believed him, and I believed that I was an excellent cook.

When I became an adult, I said to him that the broiled chicken I made could not possibly have been very good. His response was that he hated broiled chicken. I had to laugh. Looking back, I knew that it tasted awful. Even though he did not like the chicken, he was more concerned for my feelings. He could have let me know how awful my cooking really was. I would have felt crushed and discouraged and perhaps never enjoy cooking again. Instead, he praised me. Because of his encouragement, I have always loved cooking. A meek person always wants what is best for others.

Numbers 12:3 states, "Now the man Moses was very meek, above all the men which were upon the face of the earth." Psalm 19:19 tells us, "The meek also shall increase their joy in the LORD, and the poor among men shall rejoice in the Holy One of Israel."

Matthew 5:5 reads, "Blessed are the meek: for they shall inherit the earth."

Moses was the most powerful man in Israel, ruling millions of people. Yet he was the meekest man. His sister, Miriam, and brother, Aaron, wanting more recognition and power, were critical of Moses' wife. This displeased the Lord. Because of this attack, Miriam became leprous. Moses could have felt justified by this incident, yet he didn't want his sister to suffer. He wanted the best for her. He prayed, and God healed her. Moses had no need to prove his own position and power. He knew who he was in God.

Many people believe that they must be strong, hard, and unbending to survive in this world. But those that have an intimate relationship with God know that real strength comes from relying on His power. They have learned to lean on and depend on Him. Finding security in the Almighty's love and protection creates meekness. We learn how to bring out the best in others by being a conduit for God's love when we relinquish the need to control others by mental and physical force. We can become highly influential as we call others up to a higher place of living. It is not about how strong we are; it's about how powerful God is. Moses believed the best of his people, just like my dad did in me and my cooking.

Prayer

Jesus, teach me the true meaning of meekness. Teach me what real power and influence is. I desire that the character of meekness increase in me. I want to have fresh joy as the result of being meek. Amen (Ps 37:11, Is 29:19).

Soups remind me of meekness. The meek are humble, unpretentious, and yet there is more to them than meets the eye. So too are soups. Soups are made from many different ingredients, such as meat, vegetables, stock, juice, or water. They appear to be unpretentious and simple, yet they are strong in nutrition and flavor and satisfies the belly.

Soups

Albondigas Soup (Mexican Meatball Soup)

1 teaspoon olive oil
1 teaspoon onion, minced
1 clove garlic
1 8-ounce can tomato sauce
4 cups of water
2 beef bouillon cubes
2 carrots, chopped
2 stalks celery, chopped
½ cup zucchini, chopped
½ pound lean ground beef
2 tablespoons rice
1 egg
1 teaspoon salt
½ teaspoon ground pepper
3 tablespoons soft bread crumbs

Heat oil in a dutch oven. Add onion and garlic and sauté. Add tomato sauce, water, and bouillon and bring to a boil. Add carrots, celery, and zucchini. Simmer for 10 minutes. In a large mixing bowl, combine beef, bread, rice, egg, salt, and pepper. Shape into 1-inch meatballs. Carefully drop into simmering soup. Cover and cook on low heat for 25 minutes. Add more seasoning if desired.

Serves six

Minestrone Soup

½ cup onion, minced
1 garlic clove, minced
2 tablespoons parsley
1 quart water
1 quart vegetable broth
1 medium tomato, peeled, seeded, and diced
½ cup celery, diced
½ cup carrots, diced
1 medium potato, diced
1 cup spinach, diced
½ cup canned navy beans, drained
½ cup elbow macaroni, uncooked
¼ cup Parmesan cheese
Add your favorite seasonings, if you desire.

In a large pot, combine all ingredients except macaroni and cheese and bring to a boil. Add your favorite seasonings. Cover pot and simmer on low for two hours. Bring to a boil again and add macaroni and cheese. Cook about 10 minutes or until macaroni is tender.

Serves six

Mushroom Soup

4 cups chicken or vegetable broth
3 tablespoons soy sauce
1 tablespoon fresh ginger
3 garlic cloves, crushed
3 cups assorted mushrooms, such as white button, oyster, shitake (discard stems), or Portobello, cut into chunks, if needed
2 cups chicken breast, cooked and shredded
3 cups cabbage, quartered and sliced thin
2 celery stalks, sliced thin
2 cups fresh udon noodles or cooked linguine
1 cup green onions, sliced thin with green tops
2 cups baby spinach leaves
Black pepper to taste

In a dutch oven, combine broth, soy sauce, ginger, garlic, mushrooms, cabbage, celery, and chicken. Cover and bring to a boil. Simmer until mushrooms are soft, about 5 minutes. Stir in noodles, green onions, and spinach. Simmer until greens are wilted, about 2 minutes. Season to taste.

Serves six

Potato Soup

6 medium potatoes, peeled, cut in small cubes
2 leeks, chopped
2 cloves garlic, minced
2 medium onions, chopped
1 carrot, sliced
1 10½-ounce can chicken broth
4 cups water
1 tablespoon dried parsley
1 tablespoon salt
½ teaspoon pepper
⅓ cup butter or margarine
1 13-ounce can evaporated milk
Chives, chopped

In a large pot, combine all ingredients except milk and chives. Bring to a boil, and then cover pot and cook on low. Simmer for one hour. During the last 30 minutes, stir in evaporated milk, cook uncovered. When serving, sprinkle top of soup with chives.

Serves eight

Chicken and Noodle Soup

1 10½-ounce can chicken broth
4 cups water
1½ pound chicken breast, shredded
½ onion, chopped
1 clove garlic, chopped
2 medium stalks of celery, chopped
1 pound carrots, sliced
1 teaspoon salt
½ teaspoon dried thyme
¼ teaspoon pepper
1 dried bay leaf
2 cups snow peas (fresh or frozen)
2 cups uncooked wide egg noodles

In a large pot, combine chicken broth, water, and chicken and bring to a boil. Add the rest of the ingredients except snow peas and noodles. Bring to a boil, cover pot, and cook on low. Simmer for two hours. Then bring to a boil and add snow peas and noodles. Cook until the noodles are tender, about 20 minutes.

Serves six

Split Pea Soup

2 quarts water
2 cups dried green split peas
1 stalk celery, coarsely chopped
1 large carrot, chopped
1 small onion, chopped
¼ teaspoon ground thyme
1 whole bay leaf
½ teaspoon salt
½ teaspoon pepper
½ teaspoon garlic powder
½ teaspoon onion powder
2 vegetable bouillon cubes

Rinse peas thoroughly in a strainer under cold water, picking out debris and any blemished peas. In a dutch oven, combine all the ingredients and bring to a boil for 20 minutes. Cover and simmer for 30 more minutes. Remove bay leaf before serving.

Serves six

Beef Noodle Soup

1 pound lean ground beef
1 small onion, chopped
2 cloves garlic, crushed
1 14 ounce can Italian stewed tomatoes
1 6-ounce can tomato paste
1 14-ounce can beef broth
1 14-ounce can red kidney beans, drained
2 cups water
2 medium carrots, sliced
1 medium stalk celery, chopped
¼ cup green beans, cut
1 small zucchini, cut into 1-inch slices
1 small yellow squash, cut into 1-inch slices
1 teaspoon oregano
½ teaspoon salt
¼ teaspoon pepper
½ teaspoon seasoning salt
½ tablespoon parsley
½ teaspoon basil
1 cup uncooked medium egg noodles

In a large skillet, brown ground beef, onion, and garlic and then drain. Put the meat in a dutch oven. Add tomatoes, tomato paste, broth, kidney beans, water, carrots, celery, green beans, zucchini, squash, and seasonings. Bring to a boil, cover, and simmer for 40 minutes. Add noodles and cook 15 minutes or until noodles are done.

Serves six

Creamy Broccoli Rice Soup

⅓ cup water
3 cups broccoli florets, chopped
½ cup onion, chopped
1½ cups chicken stock
2 cups water
½ cup white rice
¼ teaspoon dried oregano
½ teaspoon salt
¼ teaspoon pepper

In a medium saucepan, bring ⅓ cup water to a boil over medium heat. Add broccoli and onion. Boil seven minutes or until almost tender; drain and set aside

In a dutch oven, bring chicken stock, water, and rice to a boil. Reduce heat and simmer 20 minutes or until rice is tender.

Let the broccoli and rice mixture cool down until warm. Pour into a large bowl. Place half the broccoli mixture and half the rice mixture in a food processor or blender. Cover and process until smooth. Return to the dutch oven and heat. Repeat with remaining broccoli and rice mixture. Stir in remaining ingredients and heat through.

Serves four

French Onion Soup

4 cups red or yellow onions, thinly sliced
2 cloves of garlic, minced
¼ cup butter
2 tablespoons olive oil
½ teaspoon of sugar
6 cups beef stock
1 teaspoon Worcestershire sauce
1 bay leaf
¼ teaspoon thyme
Salt and pepper to taste
6 slices french bread (¾-inch thick), buttered and toasted
1½ cups swiss cheese, grated

In a dutch oven, cook onions and garlic in butter and olive oil over medium-heat for 10 minutes. Add sugar to caramelize and simmer for 30 minutes. Add stock, Worcestershire sauce; bay leaf, thyme, salt, and pepper and bring to a boil. Reduce heat, cover and simmer 10 minutes. Remove bay leaf. Ladle hot soup into six ovenproof bowls. Top each bowl with a piece of french bread cut or tear to fit bowl. Sprinkle with cheese and broil at 350 °F for about 10 minutes or until cheese melts. Serve immediately.

Serves six

Garden Pea Soup

⅓ cup butter
¼ cup onion, minced
1 stalk celery, minced
1 carrot, minced
⅓ cup flour
4 cups chicken stock
1 tablespoon seasoned salt
¼ pound cooked ham, diced
2 cups frozen peas
2 cups light cream

In a dutch oven, melt butter and sauté onions, celery, and carrots until tender. Add the flour and cook, stirring occasionally, for two minutes. Add chicken stock, salt, ham, and peas. Simmer for ten minutes. Add the cream and simmer for an additional 10 minutes. Serve hot.

Serves six

Chapter Ten

Temperance and Salads

Many times, overeating controlled my life. Regardless of how uncomfortable it made me feel, I would not stop putting food into my mouth. Naturally, unwelcomed weight gain was the result. I was looking for comfort in the wrong place. Compulsiveness is never satisfied. No matter how much I ate, I still wanted to eat more. As I got my appetite under control, I felt much better about myself, especially the weight loss, improved health, and increased energy.

Proverbs 25:28 states, "He that hath no rule (self control) over his own spirit is like a city that is broken down and without walls." In biblical times, a city's wall was tremendously important for protection. It served as a defense for its citizens. Broken walls would allow enemies, bent on destruction, into the city. Self-control serves us in the same way. An undisciplined person who lacks self-control, opens him or herself as well as others up to trouble. When the walls are down, good escapes and evil breaks in. It becomes easy to give in to temptation, which leads to ruin. Stopping a small leak is easier than fixing a raging flood.

Compulsiveness is doing something that you do not necessarily want to do, even if it means discomfort or embarrassment. It can even lead to destruction. Compulsiveness can be conquered; self-control is a learned behavior. It takes practice, practice, and more practice. Failing does not mean giving up. We may feel uncomfortable while we practice self-control, but we press on.

When Jesus was tempted by Satan, He kept repeating the words, "It is written," proclaiming God's word to the tempter (Luke 4:1–13). He used God's Word like a sword to overcome temptation, demonstrating how we should overcome the powers of our earthly appetites. We too can use God's Word to overcome our weaknesses.

Because he was tempted yet did not give in, He understands our weaknesses. Now in heaven, He is praying that we too will overcome. We can come to Him with confidence and find mercy and grace to help us in our time of need (Hebrews 4:14–16).

Are you willing to let God help you with your weaknesses? Sometimes our feelings of inadequacy are so strong; we have a hard time trusting God's ability to help us. We must be willing and open to His help. He always does what He says He will do in His own time and way. Jesus showed how willing He was to help us, when He walked this earth. He faithfully carried out His assignment when He died for our sins. He is even faithful by praying for us right now. We know that the Father always hears Him. We trust that when our prayers are in agreement with His, God listens (Romans 8:34). He gave us His Spirit, the Holy Spirit, which is always by our side, teaching, leading, instructing us, and empowering us to overcome every obstacle.

Prayer

Jesus, teach me how to live and pray so that I will not fall into temptation. Give me the power to overcome temptation. Strengthen me to defeat Satan's power, for there is no power compared to yours. Lead me not into temptation, but deliver me from the evil one. Help me understand that no temptation is irresistible. I can trust you to keep temptation from being too strong. Amen (Matt. 26:41, 6:13, 1 Corinthians. 10:13).

Salads remind me of temperance. Self-control is about making choices. The same God that lives in us can put His strength in us to help us make good decisions about what we eat. He never grows tired of working with and helping us. He believes in us and supports us. If we fail, He is quick to restore us and point us in the right direction. Working with us to make right choices is what He loves to do.

Salads

Vegetable Salad

4 cups small cauliflower florets
1 small cucumber, sliced thin
2 cups sugar snap peas
1 small zucchini, sliced thin
½ cup red onion, minced
Shredded romaine lettuce
⅓ cup sunflower kernels
⅔ cup ranch dressing (or dressing of your choice)
Salt and pepper to taste

In a large mixing bowl, combine the cauliflower, cucumber, sugar snap peas, zucchini, red onion, and dressing. Season with salt and pepper. Layer a large serving plate with romaine lettuce. Top with vegetables. Sprinkle with sunflower seeds.

Serves six

Three Bean Salad

1 14½-ounce can green beans, drained
1 14½-ounce can garbanzo beans, drained
1 14½-ounce can kidney beans, drained
½ green pepper, diced
3 stalks celery, diced
1 small onion, diced
½ cup salad oil
½ cup balsamic vinegar
½ cup sugar
1 teaspoon salt
½ teaspoon pepper

Place the beans in a large mixing bowl along with the green pepper, celery, and onion. In medium mixing bowl, combine the oil, vinegar, sugar, salt, and pepper. Pour over the bean mixture and toss lightly. Cover and refrigerate at least two hours before serving.

Serves six

Zesty Spinach Salad

2½ ounces sliced almonds
2 bundles spinach, cleaned, drained, and separated from stems
6 slices crisp-cooked bacon
1 red apple, peeled and diced
1 green apple, peeled and diced
¼ cup red onion, chopped
2 teaspoons chives, chopped
3 hard boiled eggs, chopped
½ cup olive oil
3 tablespoons vinegar
2 teaspoons sugar
1 teaspoon dry mustard
Salt and pepper to taste

Preheat oven to 300 °F. Place almonds on a cookie sheet along with cooked bacon. Bake for 5 minutes and then set aside. After the bacon has cooled, crumble it. In a large mixing bowl, combine bacon, almonds, spinach, apples, onion, chives, and eggs. In a small mixing bowl, combine olive oil, vinegar, sugar, mustard, salt, and pepper. Pour dressing over salad and gently toss just before serving.

Serves four

Cobb Salad

6 cups romaine lettuce, torn
1 cup cooked chicken, cubed
½ cup dried cranberries
½ cup glazed pecans, halved
½ cup blue cheese, crumbled
½ cup ranch dressing
¼ cup crisp-cooked bacon, crumbled

In a large salad bowl, combine lettuce, chicken, cranberries, pecans, and blue cheese. Pour on salad dressing and toss to coat. Sprinkle with bacon.

Serves six

Taco Salad

1 pound ground beef
⅔ cup taco seasoning
1 8-ounce bag corn tortilla chips
½ head romaine lettuce, chopped
1 avocado, diced and drizzled with 2 teaspoons lemon juice
2 tomatoes, diced
1 2-½ ounce can black olives
1 14-ounce can whole kernel corn, drained
½ cup onion, chopped
2 cups shredded cheddar cheese

Cook ground beef in a large skillet over medium heat. Drain excess fat.
Stir in taco seasoning. Crumble tortilla chips on a large serving plate, layer
with lettuce, avacado, tomatoes, olives, corn, onion, beef, and cheese.

Serves six

Simple Shrimp Salad

1 pound frozen cooked shrimp
1 tablespoon olive oil
1 tablespoon butter
2 cloves garlic, sliced thin
½ cup green olives, chopped small
½ head romaine lettuce, cut or torn into bite-size pieces
½ cup shredded cheddar cheese

Thaw shrimp. Heat the oil and butter in a medium skillet over medium heat. Sauté garlic and shrimp for 5 minutes. Place romaine lettuce on serving dish. In different bowls, put the olives, shrimp, and cheese. Let each person load his or her own plate. Serve with favorite salad dressing.

Serves four

Romaine Salad with Oranges

Dressing:

1 cup ranch dressing
¼ cup orange juice concentrate
¼ cup apple juice
¼ teaspoon cinnamon

Salad:

1 large head romaine lettuce
8 mushrooms, sliced
2 cups swiss cheese, grated
1 cup seedless red grapes
1 cup fresh orange sections
½ cup sliced almonds, toasted

In a large salad bowl, combine dressing ingredients and mix well. Wash romaine lettuce, dry well, remove stems, and tear into small pieces. Place in a salad bowl and add the sliced mushrooms, cheese, grapes, and oranges. Toss and sprinkle almonds on top. Serve dressing separately.

Serves four

Chicken and Grape Salad

3 cups cooked chicken, diced
1 cup seedless green grapes
½ cup cashews
⅓ cup mayonnaise
⅓ cup lemon-flavored yogurt
3 tablespoons honey
2 teaspoons cracked pepper
6 romaine lettuce leaves
6 grape clusters

In a medium mixing bowl, combine chicken, grapes, and cashews together. In a small microwavable cup, heat honey for about 10 seconds. In a small mixing bowl, blend the mayonnaise, yogurt, honey, and pepper. Add the dressing to the chicken mixture. Arrange lettuce leaves on salad plates. Divide the salad equally on the leaves. Garnish with grape clusters.
Serves four

Chili Bean Salad

2 15-ounce cans kidney beans, drained
2 teaspoons chili powder
¼ cup olive oil
2 tablespoons vinegar
2 tablespoons sugar
¼ teaspoon salt
1 large green pepper, diced
1 small onion, diced
1 cup pitted black olives, halved
2 tablespoons salsa
1 tablespoon mayonnaise
1 small head of romaine lettuce, torn to bite-size pieces
½ cup shredded cheddar cheese

Pour beans into a large mixing bowl and set aside. In a small saucepan, heat chili powder in olive oil for 2 minutes to develop flavor; remove from heat. Stir in vinegar, sugar, and salt. Pour over beans and stir well. Let stand for 30 minutes to set flavor.

Stir in green pepper, onion, olives, salsa, and mayonnaise. Toss lightly to mix. Place romaine lettuce in a large salad bowl and spoon bean mixture on top. Top with cheese.

Serves four

Chapter Eleven

The Greatest Love

John 3:16–21 states, "God so loved the world that he gave His only begotten Son, that whosoever believeth in him should not perish, but have everlasting life. For God sent not his Son into the world to condemn the world; but that the world through him might be saved. He that believeth on him is not condemned: but he that believeth not is condemned already, because he hath not believed in the name of the only begotten Son of God."

The greatest love anyone can give is to lay down his or her life for another. Our heavenly Father demonstrated His matchless love to us through Christ, the Messiah. Jesus was totally man and totally God. He said that whoever saw Him saw the Father. He did whatever the Father told Him to do. He revealed the Father's heart when He healed the sick, raised the dead, cast demons out of people, and accepted the outcast. He fed multitudes of people. Taking on the sin of the whole world and dying a painful, torturous death on the cross has given us everlasting life. Everything Jesus did was out of love.

When I was twenty years old, I picked up a pamphlet called "The Four Spiritual Laws" from Campus Crusade for Christ. It read, "Just as there are physical laws that govern the universe, there are spiritual laws that govern your relationship with God."

The four laws go something like this:
1. God's plans for you are wonderful, as He loves you so much.
2. Man's sin separates you from knowing His love.
3. God provided Jesus Christ as the only way to know Him.
4. To know and experience God's love and plan for our lives, we must receive Jesus Christ as our Lord and Savior.

At that moment, I asked Jesus to come in to my life and wash away everything that separated me from Him. I felt peace come over me, but it took about nine months for me to really realize that Jesus is exactly who He claims to be: the only begotten Son of God, who takes away the sin of the world. He came into my life, and I have never been the same. It is the best thing that ever happened to me.

If you would like to know the love of God in a personal, intimate way, talk to Him right now. You can say, "I have lived my life separated from you. I desire to know that you deeply love me. I believe that Jesus Christ is your only begotten Son, who died under the weight of the sin of mankind so that I can come to know you. Thank you for coming into my life and setting me free."

Now start reading your Bible. The book of John is a great place to start. Visit a church and join others as they worship and learn. You will discover Jesus' loving arms are wrapped around you.

May you experience the wonderful flavor and favor of the Lord as you start your new life in Christ.

About the Author

Two great loves in Debra Brawner's life are the Lord Jesus Christ and homemaking. Although not a professional chef, she has loved working in the kitchen all her life. Experimenting with and trying new recipes is something she has enjoyed since she was a girl. She greatly enjoys cooking for family and friends. Whether it's bringing a meal to a friend, sharing recipes, or celebrating, food brings people together.

Debra loves the fellowship of other Christ-minded people. She loves the celebratory environment when believers come together to share their faith, friendship, and experiences. She also loves to comfort others with the comfort she has learned to receive from her relationship with God. Whether worshipping together, praying for each other, or ministering to others needs, faith brings people together.

Debra has been serving in a woman's ministry for twenty-five years and has loved every minute of it. She helps organize, hostess, and lead retreats and conferences. Outreach to the community, helping to feed the homeless, celebrating holidays with less fortunate children is a great delight of hers. Teaching, training, and inspiring others to live and battle life by the Word of God are a great passions of Debra's. She also serves as an elder in her church, where she teaches Bible studies.

Debra does the bookkeeping for her husband's fabrication business. Being a wife, mother, and grandmother has been one of the greatest joys (and challenges) in her life. She lives in Scottsdale, Arizona with her husband, Tom, of thirty-six years, and has three children and one grandson.